Hello and welcome!

Dein *Wordmaster*-Heft hilft dir beim Wörterlernen.

In der Schule lernst du Englisch mit dem Buch *Go Ahead 10*. Dort besprecht ihr auch die neuen Wörter einer Seite. Im Anschluss daran solltest du die Wörter im *Vocabulary* deines Schulbuchs abschnittsweise lernen.

Danach machst du zuerst die Übung **New words** in deinem *Wordmaster*-Heft, die zu der neuen Seite in deinem Englischbuch gehört. Bei dieser Aufgabe fügst du die neuen Wörter zum Beispiel in einen Text oder einen Dialog ein, oder du ordnest ihnen Definitionen zu. So übst du die neuen Wörter auf vielfältige Weise.

Wenn du einmal nicht weiterweißt, kannst du im *Unit-Vocabulary* (Wörterverzeichnis) von *Go Ahead 10* (S. 142–185) nachschauen.

Anschließend kannst du überprüfen, ob du alles richtig gelöst hast: Die Lösungen findest du im eingehefteten Lösungsteil.

Wenn du sicher bist, dass die Lösung richtig ist, präge dir die Sätze und Worterklärungen ein. So behältst du die neuen Wörter besser!

Nach **New words** bietet der *Wordmaster* noch weitere Übungen zum Lernen der neuen Wörter, zum Beispiel Lückentexte und Rätsel.

Am Ende jeder *Wordmaster-Unit* findest du dein **Learner log**, dein Lerntagebuch. Dort kannst du Fragen zu deinen Erfahrungen mit dem Wörterlernen beantworten.

Damit du überprüfen kannst, wie gut du die Wörter aus den vorigen Units noch beherrschst, gibt es an drei Stellen im *Wordmaster*-Heft *Revision*-Aufgaben: Nach Unit 2 überprüfen sie den Wortschatz der ersten beiden Units, nach Unit 4 den Wortschatz von Unit 3 und 4 und im *Finale* Wörter aus dem Gesamtwortschatz von *Go Ahead 10*. Im *Finale* gibt es auch ein großes *Go-Ahead-Quiz*.

Viel Spaß beim Englischlernen!

Go Ahead 10 – Wordmaster

Erarbeitet von:
Ursula Fleischhauer, Hannover

unter beratender Mitwirkung von:
Pia Meindl, Abensberg

in Zusammenarbeit mit der Englischredaktion:
Klaus Unger (Projektleitung), Nadja Prinz (Köln) sowie Christine Maxwell

Illustrationen:
Karen Donnelly, Brighton

Umschlaggestaltung und Layoutkonzept:
hawemannundmosch, Berlin

Layout und technische Umsetzung:
Straive, Chennai

www.cornelsen.de

1. Auflage, 1. Druck 2022

Druck: Athesiadruck GmbH, Bozen

ISBN 978-3-06-033905-1

PEFC
PEFC/04-31-1156

PEFC zertifiziert
Dieses Produkt stammt aus nachhaltig bewirtschafteten Wäldern und kontrollierten Quellen.
www.pefc.de

A diverse nation

Unit 1

1 New words SB pp. 10–11

Write the missing words in the crossword. The letters in the blue boxes form synonyms for advantages und disadvantages. You need to add a few letters to complete the synonyms.

TIP

Before you can do the exercises in this book, you need to learn the new words.

1 ►► aspect
2 the system in South Africa that gave full political rights only to white people
3 very different from each other
4 a stripe of different colours that you can sometimes see in the sky
5 a language that people with different mother tongues use to communicate with each other
6 ►► not *(a prefix you use in compounds)*
7 people living together
8 Race ??? in South Africa have improved over the last years.
9 an area which is protected for wildlife

2 Word families

Use the word given in capitals at the end of each line to form another word of the same word family that fits in the sentence.

1 Why is South Africa called a ______________ nation?	**DIVERSITY**
2 What's the ______________ between the chart and the text?	**RELATE**
3 South Africa is a multicultural ______________.	**SOCIAL**
4 These seats are ______________ for people with disabilities.	**RESERVE**

3 New words SB p. 12

a) Complete the text with the words from the box.

corruption • educational • growth • of colour • phenomenon • qualifications • reforms • weighs heavily on their shoulders • wrongs

South Africans who were born after 1990 are often called born-frees. They didn't have to suffer the **1** ______________ and injustices of apartheid but were born in times of social **2** ______________ and equal rights for all South Africans. But to this day both people **3** ______________ and whites still face a lot of problems. One of these problems is **4** ______________. It can take many forms, e.g. civil servants asking for money in exchange for services, or politicians giving money or jobs to their sponsors, friends or family. Of course, this does not only happen in South Africa – it's a **5** ______________ you can see all over the world. Another problem is South Africa's slow economic **6** ______________ which is responsible for its high youth unemployment rate. A good **7** ______________ system could bring change, but that would mean putting a lot of money into schools. Young people need good **8** ______________ to find jobs. Young black South Africans often support their parents financially which **9** ______________.

b) Match the words (A–I) with the corresponding definitions (1–11). Write the correct numbers in the grid below. Be careful: There are two definitions that you don't need.

A optimistic
B (to) agree (on)
C youth
D nanny
E (to) struggle
F diploma
G entrepreneur
H beyond
I (to) fix

1 ►► the time when you are young; a young man
2 a document which shows that you have completed a part of your education
3 a small child
4 ►► (to) fight
5 ►► on the other side
6 ◄► pessimistic
7 successful
8 ►► (to) repair
9 a person who looks after other people's children in their home
10 (to) decide together on an idea
11 ►► businessman/businesswoman

A	B	C	D	E	F	G	H	I

4 Prepositions

Complete the sentences with the right preposition from the box.

about • for • in • of • on

1 Before Cindy can buy things for herself, she needs to think ______________ her parents.

2 To correct the wrongs ______________ apartheid, many jobs in South Africa are now reserved ______________ people of colour.

3 ______________ 2020 South Africa had the highest youth unemployment rate in the world.

4 Kevin thinks applicants should be judged ______________ their skills, not their skin colour.

5 New words SB p. 13

Complete the sentences with the words from the box.

at times • fail • grasp • largely • not necessarily • party • provinces • racism • similarities • socialize • township • wrestle

1 Soweto is a ________________ outside Johannesburg. It is still ________________ the home of black South Africans.

2 South Africa has nine ________________. Gauteng, where Kevin du Plessis lives, is the smallest and most crowded one.

3 The cruelty and injustices of apartheid are still hard to ________________.

4 ________________ kept people of different skin colour apart. Blacks and whites didn't ________________.

5 Although laws in modern South Africa are aimed at equality, racist views have ________________ disappeared and people of colour still ________________ with them. Some whites still see more differences than ________________ between themselves and black South Africans.

6 The ANC is South Africa's majority ________________.

7 Cindy Mfabe feels responsible for her parents. She works hard because she doesn't want to ________________ them. ________________ this is putting a lot of pressure on her.

6 Word families

Use the word given in capitals at the end of each line to form another word of the same word family that fits in the sentence.

1 Lack of light will stop the plants' ________________.	GROW
2 Samuel is a ________________ teacher.	QUALIFICATION
3 Children don't want to ________________ their parents.	FAILURE
4 ________________ is a huge problem in many societies.	RACIST

7 New words SB p. 14

Write the missing words in the crossword.

1 Paul likes music, ??? hip hop.
2 Kungawo wants to be a pantsula dancer. He often practises new ???.
3 Moving into their own accommodation is an important ??? in people's lives.
4 Shirts, skirts and trousers are pieces of ???.
5 Martha's legs hurt, so she ??? slowly from her bed to the bathroom.
6 Hip hop music has a fast ??? beat.
7 ►► (to) react, (to) answer
8 *across:* a total change in the way of doing things (the Industrial / French ???)
8 *down:* The new take-away restaurant sells an endless ??? of soups and salads.
9 ►► (to) put your foot down very hard
10 (to) move sth. from one place to another
11 (to) turn sth. strongly
12 verb: (to) resist – noun: ???
13 There is a speed ??? of 120 km/h on South African national roads.
14 a strong wish or need to do sth.
15 ◄► outer

8 New words SB p. 15

Jonas from Germany is on a school exchange in Johannesburg. He has seen an advert for the musical Abantu. His exchange partner Thato tells him what Abantu is about.
Complete the dialogue with the words from the box.

celebration • chained • choreographer • combined • era • gumboot • hardship • hurry • rural • slapped • stomped

Jonas: I saw an advert today for the musical Abantu. Do you think we can get tickets for it?

Thato: They are usually sold out very quickly, but if we **1** ________________, we might be lucky to get some. Have you heard of Abantu?

Jonas: No, I haven't. What is it?

Thato: It's a dance style that was developed in the **2** ________________ of apartheid. **3** ________________ men – you know, men from the country – created it. As they wore special kinds of boots it's also called the **4** ________________ dance.

Jonas: Interesting. Is there a story behind it?

Thato: There is: These men had come to Johannesburg hoping to find a better life working in the gold mines, but working conditions there were horrible. The men were **5** ________________ together and not allowed to talk.
They really suffered **6** ________________.

Jonas: And still danced?

Thato: Well, they clapped their hands, **7** ________________ their bodies and **8** ________________ their feet. **9** ________________ with traditional tribal and European dances a new dance was born.

Jonas: That sounds really interesting. Have you heard of Paul Nkuma, the **10** ________________ of the musical?

Thato: I have. He's quite famous. One gets the impression that for him Abantu is the **11** ________________ of song and dance.

9 New words SB p. 16

a) *Write the missing words in the crossword. The letters in the blue boxes form a word that you use when something causes angry public discussion and disagreement.*

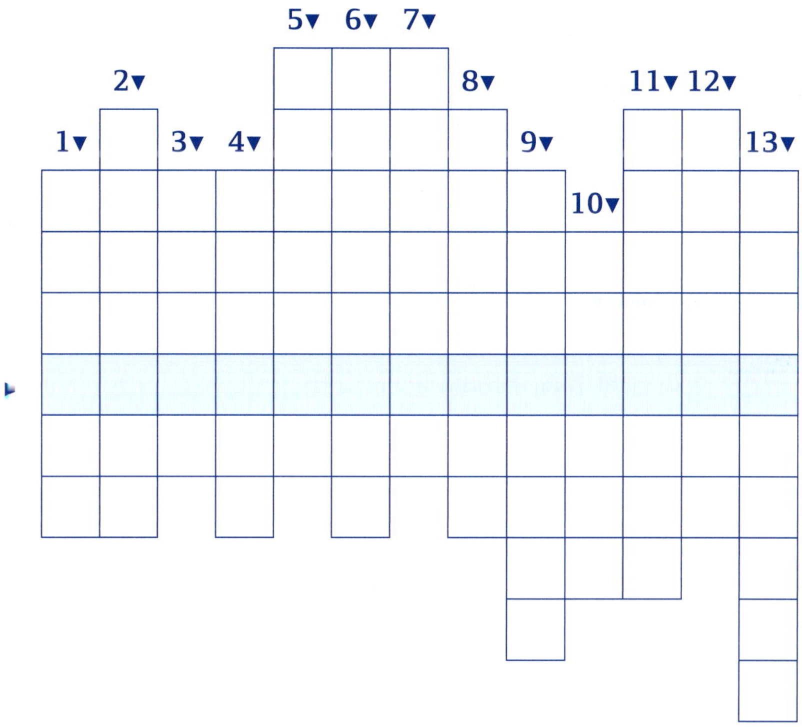

1

3

5

12

2 (to) shut a place in on all sides
4 ►► cruel, violent
6 ►► from birth until death
7 kept in a space from which one cannot escape
8 ►► diversity
9 a person or a company that runs a business
10 the act of saving sb./sth. from a dangerous situation
11 qualities people or animals are born with that make them behave in a certain way
13 in every country on earth

b) *Complete the sentences with the words from the box.*

active • informative • questionable • radically • widespread

1 An ____________________ lifestyle is good for people's health, but they shouldn't change their lives too ____________________.

2 The floods caused ____________________ damage in the area, but rebuilding the houses in the same places is a very ____________________ idea.

3 The magazine contains lots of ____________________ articles on the effects of climate change.

c) Match the words (A–O) with the corresponding definitions (1–15). Write the correct numbers in the grid below.

A ... as well as ...
B (to) breed
C canned hunting
D cub
E game
F habitat
G initiative
H (to) nurse
I petition
J (to) poach
K practice
L (to) profit (from)
M rehabilitation
N (to) return
O to the wild

1 shooting animals in enclosed areas of which they can't escape
2 a plan to achieve a certain purpose
3 (to) illegally hunt birds, animals or fish
4 (to) care for an animal or person that is ill
5 a certain way of doing sth.
6 the process of nursing a person or an animal to health so that they can go back to their normal lives
7 (to) get sth. useful or precious from a situation
8 ►► to the wilderness
9 ►► and also
10 (to) keep animals to produce young ones
11 the place where an animal or plant is normally found
12 ►► (to) give back; (to) go back
13 wild animals or the meat of wild animals
14 a written document signed by a large number of people who want sth. they think is important to be changed
15 a young bear, lion, tiger, etc.

A	B	C	D	E	F	G	H	I	J	K	L	M	N	O

10 Antonyms

Write words that mean the opposite.

1 optimistic ◄► ________________
2 right ◄► ________________
3 difference ◄► ________________
4 active ◄► ________________
5 slow ◄► ________________
6 bright ◄► ________________
7 advantage ◄► ________________
8 available ◄► ________________
9 huge ◄► ________________
10 majority ◄► ________________

11 New words SB p. 17

a) Complete the dialogue with the words from the box.

air conditioning • circumstances • in fact • partial • refund

Is there no **1** ____________________ in this room? It's very hot in here.

2 ____________________ there is, but it doesn't seem to be working.

Under these **3** ____________________ I would like to move into another room.

I'm afraid we're fully booked, but I can offer you a **4** ____________________

5 ____________________ of the room rate – 700 Rand instead of 1360 Rand.

b) Complete the sentences with the words from the box.

complaint • consequences • demand • elaborate • formulate • little • prompts • receipt

If something you bought isn't working properly, you can send a written **1** ____________________ to the company that sold it to you. **2** ____________________ a friendly email and attach a copy of the **3** ____________________ of the object you bought. Inform the company about the problems you have with the object and either **4** ____________________ a new one or ask to get your money back. Explain the **5** ____________________ there might be if the company is not willing to refund you. If you find writing such an email difficult, write down some **6** ____________________ first and **7** ____________________ on them later. Don't forget: Most young people know very **8** ____________________ about their consumer rights.

12 New words SB p. 18

a) What are these people's jobs? Write them on the lines under the pictures.

1 ______________________ 2 ______________________ 3 ______________________

b) Match the words (A–K) with the corresponding definitions (1–13). Write the correct numbers in the grid below. Be careful: There are two definitions that you don't need.

A comprehension
B fine
C face to face
D genuine
E homeland
F pandemonium
G political
H (to) take a right/left
I unique
J whenever
K (to) yell (at)

1 connected with any public affairs or the government
2 any time you want
3 ►► (to) shout loudly at sb.
4 to help someone to improve their situation
5 ►► (to) turn right/left
6 ►► looking at each other
7 the ability to understand
8 the country where sb. was born
9 ►► not like anything else
10 money you must pay for breaking a law or rule
11 a musical instrument
12 ►► real
13 ►► chaos

A	B	C	D	E	F	G	H	I	J	K

c) Complete the sentences with the words from the box.

clue • dock • equated with • get away with • a leg up • intelligence • light-skinned • option • would yell

1 Tom is very ______________________. He needs to be very careful in the sun.

2 Speaking foreign languages will give you ______________________ when you look for a job.

3 Mariam doesn't have a ______________________ who stole her mobile phone.

4 A job in the computer industry is often ______________________ a high salary.

5 Professors are seen as people with a high ______________________.

6 Dylan thought he would ______________________ selling stolen bikes, but he didn't.

7 When Dylan sat in the ______________________ and was told by the judge that he would have to pay a fine, he was angry with himself.

8 People in small villages often have no other ______________________ than getting a job in a bigger place.

9 When other children saw Noah, they ______________________ "the white man" at him.

13 Synonyms

Using a word from the box, rewrite each sentence so that it has a similar meaning to the first sentence.

rural area • educational • large • (to) take a right • worldwide

1 English is spoken all over the world.

____

2 Shawn has grown up on a farm with lots of fields around it.

____

3 To get to the station you have to turn right at the cinema and then go straight on.

____

4 The Johnsons live in a really big house.

____

5 Sally only watches TV programmes that provide useful information or knowledge.

____

14 New words SB p. 19

Write the missing words in the crossword. The explanations are below the crossword and on the next page.

1 (to) bring sb. food or drinks

2 (to) deal with a situation in a certain way

3 a line that divides two places

4 (to) be ??? in sth. = (to) have a good knowledge of sth.

5 (to) say the way that a ship, plane, car, etc. must go

6 *across:* an informal word for "man"

6 *down:* a person who owns a shop

7 Children often ??? up words and expressions they don't really understand.

8 If you are ??? for sth., you show strong feelings for it.
9 If sth. causes ???, it is making people uncertain about sth.
10 If a South African person says, "I'm going to hit you ??? your head", they mean they're going to hit you on your head.
11 ►► only
12 (to) treat sb. in an unfair way, especially by not giving them the same freedom, rights, etc. as other people
13 sth. that happens
14 (to) attack sb. in a public place and steal things from them
15 ►► short
16 ►► badly behaved *(especially said about children)*
17 (to) describe the character of sth. or sb.
18 a small animal that can change its colour according to what is around it
19 a person who acts in a stupid way
20 the way you notice things with your senses
21 able to speak, read and write a (foreign) language well

15 Verbs and nouns

Read the sentences. Some verbs and nouns look the same. Circle the nouns and underline the verbs.

1 Tom doubts that his train will be on time. The conductor said he would get his connecting train, but Tom had his doubts.
2 Lots of people struggle with spelling. Some believe they have lost the struggle.
3 Lucy always counts her steps when she walks to school. Sometimes she steps into nasty things.
4 Some people don't know their limits when they drink alcohol. The law limits the alcoholic drinks that may be sold to people under 18.
5 Ahmad and Samira had to hurry to catch their bus. They were in such a hurry that they forgot their lunch boxes at home.
6 Three young people helped to rescue the lion cubs from the fire. One of them helps in a rescue centre for wild animals at the weekend.
7 Junior nurses sick animals in his free time. His two older sisters are nurses at the local hospital.
8 There has been a shift in people's attitude towards climate change. But some people try to shift people's attention away from things that need to be done about it.
9 The workers' demand for a higher pay seems reasonable. Some workers also demand higher safety standards.

16 New words SB p. 20

Complete the sentences with the words from the box.

architect • barriers • effort • physical

1 During the corona pandemic people were asked to reduce ______________________ contact with other people.

2 The museum was designed by a famous ______________________.

3 The spectators had to stand behind the safety ______________________.

4 Lesedi made a big ______________________ to pass his driving test.

17 New words SB p. 21

Complete the sentences with the correct words.

Thambo is in a very bad **1** ______________________ today.

I really love the **2** ______________________ in this cinema. What's the **3** ______________________ of the film we're going to watch?

18 New words SB p. 22

Complete the sentences with the words from the box.

clarify • in other words • misunderstandings • put • rephrase

Communicating with people can sometimes lead to **1** ______________________. If this happens, try to **2** ______________________ what you've said or understood, or ask the other person to **3** ______________________ what he or she means. Stay calm, **4** ______________________, don't panic, and try to **5** ______________________ what you want to say in another way.

19 Synonyms

Read the sentences and find a word in the box that has the same meaning as the underlined word.

at times • brief • entrepreneur • merely • mostly • youths

1 The hotel is largely booked by rich people. ________

2 Ivan said nothing, only smiled and waited for Luana's reaction. ________

3 You don't have to write a long letter. A short answer will do. ________

4 Timor started off with a small shop. Now he is a successful businessman. ________

5 Lots of young men were hanging out waiting for something to happen. ________

6 Sometimes Noah felt very lonely and didn't know what to do. ________

My learner log

Mein Lerntagebuch. Hier notierst du deine Erfahrungen mit dem Wörterlernen.

★ My three favourite words in this unit are:

____

I can …

- understand basic information about South Africa. *(Write three words that are often used to describe the facets of South Africa.)*

____

____

- analyze a short film and write a film review. *(Write three words you need to write a film review.)*

____

What was difficult in Unit 1:

____

What was easy in Unit 1:

____

What I liked about Unit 1:

____

Unit 2

Aotearoa – New Zealand

1 New words SB pp. 26–27

Read the definitions and write the words from the box next to them.

census • cloud • Commonwealth • doubtful • ethnic • flightless • format • icon • insight • kiwi • marine • Pacific Islands • peninsula • sheep

1 a bird that can't fly and only lives in New Zealand: ______

2 an area of land that is widely surrounded[1] by water but joined to a larger piece of land: ______

3 the design of sth., e.g. an exam or a TV program: ______

4 a white or grey mass in the sky: ______

5 a person, animal or thing that people see as a symbol: ______

6 an organization of 54 countries which used to be part of the British Empire: ______

7 areas of land in the world's biggest and deepest ocean: ______

8 belonging to a group of people that share a cultural tradition: ______

9 unable to fly *(said of birds or insects)*: ______

10 an animal that is kept on farms for its milk, meat or wool: ______

11 the official counting of something, especially a country's population: ______

12 not sure, uncertain: ______

13 an understanding of what something is like: ______

14 connected with the ocean and the animals and plants that live there: ______

[1] (to) surround *umgeben*

2 New words SB p. 28

a) Complete the caption under each picture with a word or expression from the box.

British Isles • cup • ~~gear~~ • laughing their heads off • ritual • ~~tackling~~

1 Putting on one's rugby gear

2 tackling another player

3 Presenting the cup

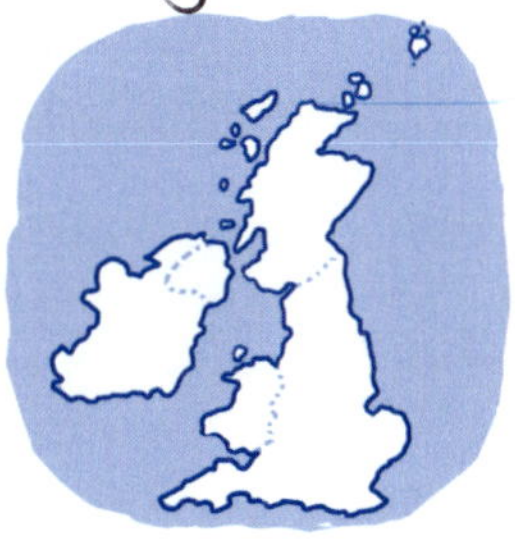

4 The British Isles

5 Two teens laughing their heads of

6 A father and son Sunday ritual: jogging through the park

b) Read the sentences and complete them with the words from the box.

grassroots • ideals • impressive • integral • mentality • psyche • ties • tough • turning point

1 Sports is an integral part of many British schools.

2 Local clubs need support at impressive level.

3 It's difficult to understand the ~~psyche~~ grassroots of people who hit their children.

4 Rugby is a ~~tough~~ tough game. Players often get hurt.

5 Getting a permanent job marked a turning point in Kyra's life.

6 It's not always easy to live up to one's mentality.

7 Lorna still keeps strong ties with her friends and family.

8 Watching horror films is not good for young children's psyche.

9 New Zealand set an ideals ~~impressive~~ ~~integral~~ example in fighting the corona pandemic.

c) Match the words (A–M) with the corresponding definitions (1–15). Write the correct numbers in the grid below. Be careful: There are two definitions that you don't need.

A (a)round the world
B (to) catch on
C characteristic (of)
D (to) frame
E gathering
F historian
G hub
H importance
I nationwide
J opponent
K (to) run deep
L original
M (to) shape (sth. into sth.)

1 sb. who studies history and is an expert in it
2 all over the country, everywhere in the country
3 (to) be felt in a strong way; (to) have a long tradition
4 (to) get on a bus
5 ►► (to) form sth., (to) build sth.
6 a meeting of people for a particular reason
7 ►► typical (of)
8 ►► all over the world
9 an important / a central airport, train station, etc.
10 sb. you fight or play against; sb. you argue with
11 (to) put sth. around a picture
12 of great value
13 the act of putting your arms around sb.
14 ►► (to) become very popular
15 the earliest; sth. that is real and not a copy

A	B	C	D	E	F	G	H	I	J	K	L	M
8	14	7	11	6	1	9	12	2	10	3	15	5

3 Word families: adjectives and nouns

Complete the table with the English and German words.

	adjective	in German	noun	in German
1	cloudy	wolkig	cloud	Wolke
2	doubtfull	zweifelhaft, ungewiss	doubt	Zweifel
3	important	wichtig, bedeutungsvoll	importance	Wichtigkeit
4	impressive	beeindruckend	Impression	Eindruck
5	intelligent	intelligent	intelligence	Intelligenz

4 New words SB p. 29

Read the text and complete it with the words from the box.

function • highly • powerful • rivals • sidelines • teammates • Union

Kaia and Aroha have been 1 teammates for three years. Before that time, they played for two different teams and were 2 rivals on the rugby field.

Ari plays for a local Rugby 3 Union club. Last week he broke his leg. Now he is watching a match from the 4 sidelines. He hopes to return to the rugby field soon. His team has an important social 5 function in his village. It's 6 highly professional and its coach is a very 7 powerfull person in the community.

5 Word families

Use the word given in capitals at the end of each line to form another word of the same word family that fits in the sentence.

1 Bright colours are ______ features of her paintings.	CHARACTER
2 Many people missed family ______ during the pandemic.	GATHER
3 Not everybody likes to be asked about their ______ background by strangers.	ETHNICITY
4 Salads and soups are ______ suited for a potluck dinner.	IDEAL

6 New words SB p. 30

Write the missing words in the crossword.

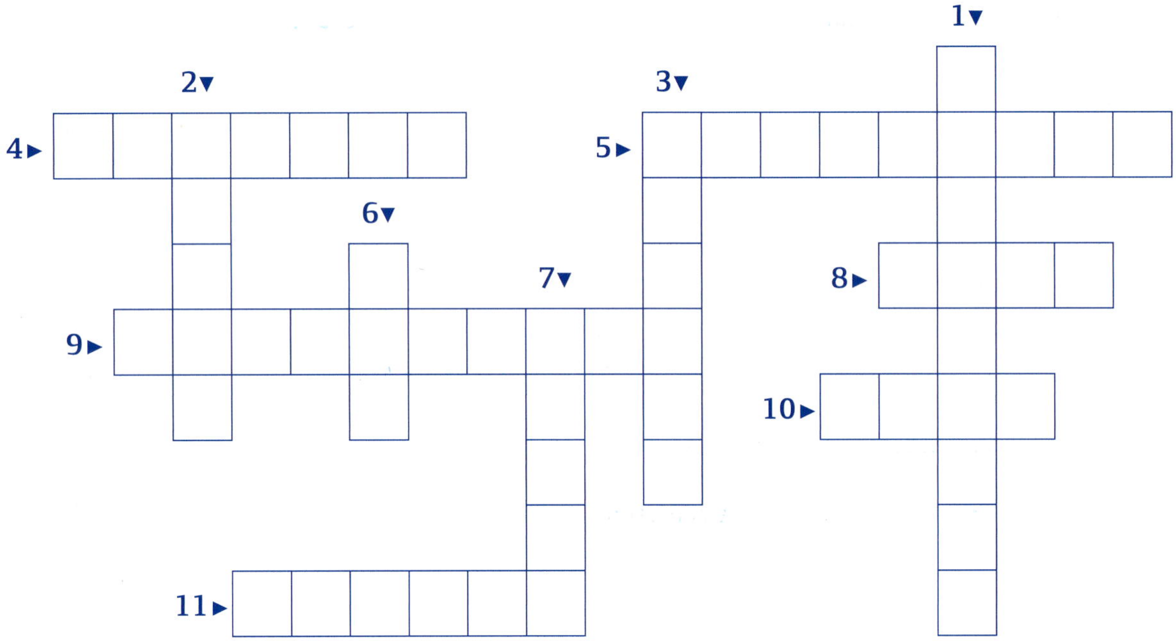

1 ►► extremely funny

2 ??? Cook is New Zealand's highest mountain.

3 ►► rude in a funny or annoying way

4 Nina and Taika used to be really good friends, but they ??? lost touch.

5 We can't say with any ??? whether you will get the job.

6

7 a ??? of kids

8 You're not allowed to ??? in the wild in Germany.

9 ►► hard to believe

10 ►► very good, impressive or great fun

11 Her ??? smelt of garlic.

7 New words SB p. 31

Read the sentences and complete them with the words from the box.

absolutely • bumped into • spins and turns • headed • locations • otherwise • she has a point • straight • universe

Hi Mum and Dad, I just wanted to let you know that I have arrived safely in New Zealand. The flight was OK, and guess what: When I left the airport, I **1** ____________ Gemma, an old friend from school. Together we **2** ____________ **3** ____________ for Queenstown to find a hostel. Gemma wants to rest for a few days before going to Mt Aspiring National Park. I think **4** ____________, and I'll stay with her **5** ____________ we'll be too exhausted for the trip we're planning to do. Remember how I used to love the *Lord of the Rings* films? Gemma and I want to visit a few **6** ____________ where they were filmed. We don't know yet what we want to do after that, but Queenstown is said to be the **7** ____________ for adventure sport, so I'm sure we're going to find lots of great things. Gemma wants to go on a jetboat journey, but I won't join her because I know they do **8** ____________, and I'd get **9** ____________ sick on the boat.

8 New words SB p. 32

a) Label the pictures with the words from the box.

campsite • canyon • kayak • sandals • swimwear • swings

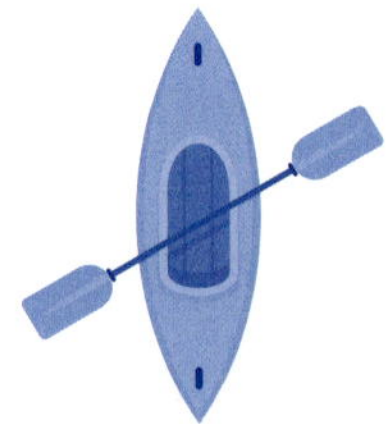

1 ____________ 2 ____________ 3 ____________

4 ____________ *(BE)* 5 ____________ 6 ____________

b) Read the sentences and complete them with the words from the box.

commercial • bring along • get informed about • the gist of • guided tour • paddle • recharge • strapped • sunblock

1 Lots of tourists prefer going on a ____________ to walking around by themselves.

2 Before you apply for a job ____________ the requirements.

3 The speaker talked so fast that most people didn't even understand ____________ what he was saying.

4 The hotel offers canoes which the guests can hire to ____________ around the lake.

5 Kayakers need to protect their skin with a good ____________.

6 The *Lord of the Rings* films were a big ____________ success.

7 He ____________ his bag onto his bike so that it couldn't fall off.

8 Where can I ____________ my phone?

9 The show is open to everyone. ____________ your friends or family.

9 New words SB p. 33

Match the words (A–I) with the corresponding definitions (1–11). Write the correct numbers in the grid below. Be careful: There are two definitions that you don't need.

A (to) admit
B expressive
C lovely
D (to) signal
E spectacular
F spot
G stylistic
H unexpected
I unless

1 a particular area or place; a small dirty mark on sth.
2 ►► (to) show, (to) make clear
3 noun: style – adjective: ???
4 used to give the only situation in which something will not happen or be true
5 ►► different
6 surprising because you didn't think it would happen
7 showing your thoughts and feelings
8 ►► very impressive
9 (to) agree that sth. is true
10 ►► (to) lie
11 ►► beautiful, attractive; very kind

A	B	C	D	E	F	G	H	I

10 Synonyms

Find the word in the box that can replace one word in the sentence without changing the meaning. In sentences 1 and 2, the words you need to replace are underlined. In sentences 3–5, you need to find the words yourself.

campground • gear • highly • hilarious • rivals

1 Although they were friends, they were political <u>opponents</u>. ______________
2 It had rained all day so that all their <u>equipment</u> was wet. ______________
3 The show was very funny. ______________
4 The show was also very professional. ______________
5 It was getting late, and they hadn't found a campsite yet. ______________

11 New words SB p. 34

Write the missing words in the crossword. The explanations are on the next page.

1 Watch what you're saying and choose your words with ???.

2 a short journey made for pleasure, e.g. a school ???

3 (to) put clothes on yourself or on somebody

4 a feature or a service that makes a place pleasant (e.g. a shop, a station, a library)

5 ►► spirit

6 Keanu's parents had no ??? against his plan to spend a year abroad.

7 If you want to lose weight, you should ??? ??? on fat and sugar.

8 More and more young people want to be actively ??? in politics.

9 (to) break sth. into very small pieces

10 The boy was born with ??? feet so that he needed special shoes later in life.

11 ►► somehow

12 a person or company that makes profit from buying land to develop it

13 Patricia Grace's ??? *Potiki* was first published in 1986.

14 ►► should, (to) be supposed to

15 near a coast

16 Our teacher didn't want to go on a class trip, but in the end, we managed to ??? her.

17 ►► (for) the time being

18 When the old man fell, he couldn't get up on his ??? again.

19 (to) make as small as possible

20 Tom cut his finger on a ??? knife.

21 difficult to understand or explain; strange

22 ►► (to) work together

23 (to) make sb. happy

24 the ability to predict what could happen, and to prepare for it appropriately

12 New words SB p. 35

a) Read the sentences and complete them with the words from the box.

blasted • central • cost • craft • feel sorry for • forehead • furious • in favour of • interest • lined with • means • rotate • along with

1 Kendo gave up football ____________________ rugby.

2 The ____________________ reached the harbour twenty minutes delayed.

3 Our family needs a new car, but we don't have the ____________________ to buy one.

4 Tyra's house is very ____________________ so that she can walk to the theatre, all the shops and the railway station.

5 There was a loud noise when the helicopter's blades started to ____________________.

6 It's not always easy to ____________________ young people in politics.

7 The ____________________ of food has gone up recently.

8 Fridays for Future activists ____________________ Scientists for Future demand faster action against climate change.

9 The workers ____________________ a big hole in the rock to build a tunnel.

10 In the summer our village roads are ____________________ lots of flowers.

11 Suri's brother was ____________________ when she broke his mobile phone.

12 Lorna has a bad headache because she hit her ____________________ on a shelf.

13 We ____________________ our neighbours whose house was badly damaged in last night's storm.

b) Write captions underneath each picture, using a word from the box.

be seated • dynamite • flames • granny's • seeds

① 
Putting ________ in the ground

② 
Waiting to ____________

③ 

Decorating ____________ birthday cake

④ 
Trying to put out the ____________

⑤ 
50 tons of ____________, and the house is gone

13 New words SB p. 36

Match the words (A–O) with the corresponding definitions (1–17). Write the correct numbers in the grid below. Be careful: There are two definitions that you don't need.

A (all) at once
B anger
C (to) bend
D (to) carve
E (to) conclude
F domain
G enslavement
H gentle
I hymn
J murmur
K perspective
L release
M scramble (for)
N sorrow
O (to) wipe

1 a brown animal that lives in the mountains
2 (to) push and fight with others to get sth. or to get to a place
3 ►► calm and kind
4 (to) decide or believe something as a result of what you have heard or seen
5 area of knowledge where sb. is an expert
6 a way of seeing things or thinking about things
7 ►► (to) hit
8 the feeling of being very sad
9 (to) rub sth. with a cloth to clean or dry it
10 ►► immediately
►► at the same time
11 the state of being set free
12 the strong feeling that you have when something has happened that you think is bad and unfair
13 the act of making somebody a slave
14 (to) make patterns into wood, etc. by cutting away material
15 a religious song, especially one praising God that is sung by Christians in church
16 (to) lean in a particular direction
17 a quietly spoken word or words

A	B	C	D	E	F	G	H	I	J	K	L	M	N	O

14 Odd word out

Circle the odd word out.

1 opponent – historian – rival – enemy

2 sheep – kea – kiwi – seed

3 importance – impressive – incredible – likeable

15 New words SB p. 37, p. 162

Read the sentences and complete them with the right words from the box.

rebuilding • rediscovered • reset • reuse

1 I'll ______________ your printer, Granny, and it'll work again after that.

2 Sam and Jane have ______________ standard dance.

3 The Coxes are ______________ their house which was damaged in the storm.

4 Try to avoid plastic bags, and if you can't, at least ______________ them.

16 Word families

Use the word given in capitals at the end of each line to form another word of the same word family that fits in the sentence.

1 I ______________ agree with you.	ABSOLUTE
2 I have never heard that ______________ before.	EXPRESS
3 Can I ______________ you to come to my party?	PERSUASION

17 New words SB p. 38

Write the missing words in the crossword. The letters in the blue boxes form the word you use to describe something that is so bad that it shouldn't be allowed.

1 (to) speak angrily with sb.
2 ►► not (well-)known
3 (to) learn or achieve sth. completely
4 (to) try to be aware of what's happening around you to avoid danger
5 a disease that spreads over a whole country or the whole world
6 expecting a baby
7 used to describe ordinary people in general
8 ►► many (different)
9 a very strong feeling for sth., often shared by many people at the same time
10 very nice and easy to like
11 happening once a week or every week
12 sb. who uses violence to achieve political aims or to force a government to act

18 Key word transformation

Rewrite each sentence so that it has a similar meaning to the first sentence, using the word or words given in capitals. Do not change the word(s) in capitals.

1 Jim's parents had no objections to his plan to study abroad. *(TO) OBJECT*

____

2 Laura and her parents often argue about her loud music. *REGULAR ARGUMENTS*

____

3 You will find information about Māori traditions on the internet. *(TO) GET INFORMED*

____

4 Nobody knew that she was pregnant. *PREGNANCY*

____

My learner log

Mein Lerntagebuch. Hier notierst du deine Erfahrungen mit dem Wörterlernen.

★ My three favourite words in this unit are:

____

I can …

- understand some Māori words. *(Write two examples.)* ______________________________
- use some idioms. *(Write two examples.)* ______________________________

What was difficult in Unit 2:

____

What was easy in Unit 2:

____

What I liked about Unit 2:

____

Revision: Units 1 & 2

1 Antonyms

Write words that mean the opposite.

1 pessimistic ◂▸ ____________________
2 different ◂▸ ____________________
3 acceptable ◂▸ ____________________
4 passive ◂▸ ____________________

2 What are they doing?

Write what the people in the pictures are doing.

1 Liam is ____________ his foot because he's angry.

2 Lea is ____________ at her brother.

3 The man is ____________ customers in a restaurant.

4 They are ____________ by a river.

5 Leila is ____________ her phone.

6 Jared is ____________ his baby into the car seat.

3 Verbs

Circle the right verb in each sentence.

1 Some political decisions are hard to weigh / grasp / conclude.
2 Our friends breed / bred / handle border collies.
3 Take / Turn / Give a right after the theatre.
4 After the show had ended, people shouted / scrambled / stamped for the exit.
5 The class tried to persuade / promise / impress their teacher to watch a film with them.
6 If your printer doesn't work, try to recharge / reuse / reset it.

4 Adjectives

Write the eight adjectives next to the correct description.

lifelong • lovely • multiple • nationwide • partial • pregnant • rural • widespread

1 relating to the countryside: ____________________

2 from when you're born until you die: ____________________

3 existing in a large area or among lots of people: ____________________

4 not completely: ____________________

5 all over the country: ____________________

6 expecting a baby: ____________________

7 many (different): ____________________

8 beautiful, wonderful: ____________________

5 Word families

Use the word given in capitals at the end of each line to form another word of the same word family that fits in the sentence.

1 Be careful about what you publish on ____________ media.	SOCIETY
2 Mr Cox was very ____________ about the broken window.	ANGER
3 The two parties finally reached an ____________.	AGREE
4 ____________ is a problem in lots of countries.	RACIST
5 The audience clapped their hands ____________.	RHYTHM
6 The film was produced in ____________ with the local theatre.	COOPERATE
7 Martha was an ____________ creative woman.	INCREDIBLE
8 Please treat the furniture with ____________.	CAREFUL

Into the world

Unit 3

1 New words SB pp. 42–43

Write the English words in the gaps.

au pair • budgeting • gap • heating • I can't wait • ironing • make up my mind • managed • overspend • placemats • run out of money • term • tidying up • Yippee

I'd planned to take a **1** ____________ year after school, but unfortunately, I haven't **2** ____________ to save enough money for the flight. I didn't earn anything during **3** ____________ time, and **4** ____________ is not one of my strengths. I often **5** ____________ on clothes. Now I need to **6** ____________ about what I want to do instead.

7 ____________! School's over! Next month I'll start an internship with an IT company. **8** ____________! If I get a job there later, I will never **9** ____________ again.

I found a family in Oslo who needs an **10** ____________ for their two young children. I'm good with children and I don't mind **11** ____________ their rooms. I hope I won't have to do any **12** ____________. I also hope their house has good **13** ____________. Winters will be cold in Norway. I bought four **14** ____________ showing Munich as a present for them.

2 New words SB p. 44

a) Match the words (A–I) with the corresponding definitions (1–11). Write the correct numbers in the grid below. Be careful: There are two definitions that you don't need.

A (to) assist (with)
B candidate
C essential
D (to) hatch
E (to) immerse
F partly
G (to) renovate
H resident
I (to) strengthen

1 ►► very important
2 someone who lives in a particular place which is their home
3 (to) become completely involved in something
4 ◄► completely
5 (to) repair an old building or flat so that it looks good
6 ►► very big
7 someone who is applying for a job or is taking part in a game show
8 (to) come out of an egg *(e.g. birds, turtles)*
9 using strength to fight something
10 ►► (to) help (with)
11 (to) make sb./sth. stronger; (to) become stronger

A	B	C	D	E	F	G	H	I

b) Read the sentences and complete them with a word from the box.

backgrounds • disadvantaged • hands-on • in order to • meet

1 A lot of community centres in Britain offer groups and classes for people from different ________________.
2 People who ________________ the necessary requirements get a reduced fee.
3 Students from ________________ families find help with their schoolwork there.
4 Other classes offer ________________ computer training and drawing or sewing classes.
5 For some of these classes people need to apply early ________________ get a place.

GO»
AHEAD
REALSCHULE BAYERN

Wordmaster

10

Lösungen

1 A diverse nation

1 New words SB pp. 10–11

Solution: the pros and cons

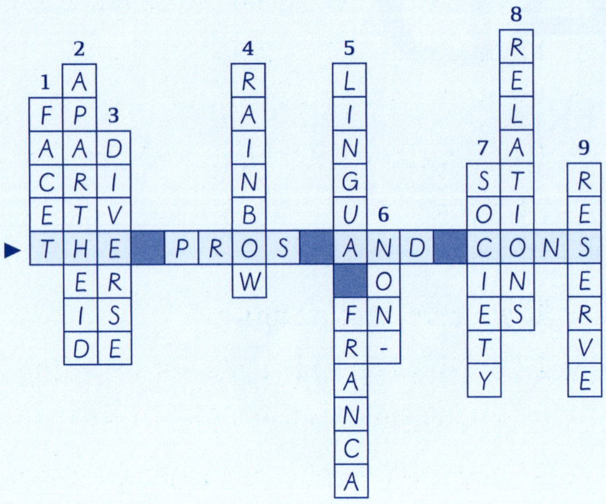

2 Word families

1 diverse **2** relation **3** society **4** reserved

3 New words SB p. 12

a)

1 wrongs **2** reforms **3** of colour **4** corruption **5** phenomenon **6** growth **7** educational **8** qualifications **9** weighs heavily on their shoulders

b)

A 6 **B** 10 **C** 1 **D** 9 **E** 4 **F** 2 **G** 11 **H** 5 **I** 8

4 Prepositions

1 about **2** of; for **3** In **4** on

5 New words SB p. 13

1 township; largely **2** provinces **3** grasp **4** Racism; socialize **5** not necessarily; wrestle; similarities **6** party **7** fail; At times

6 Word families

1 growth **2** qualified **3** fail **4** Racism

7 New words SB p. 14

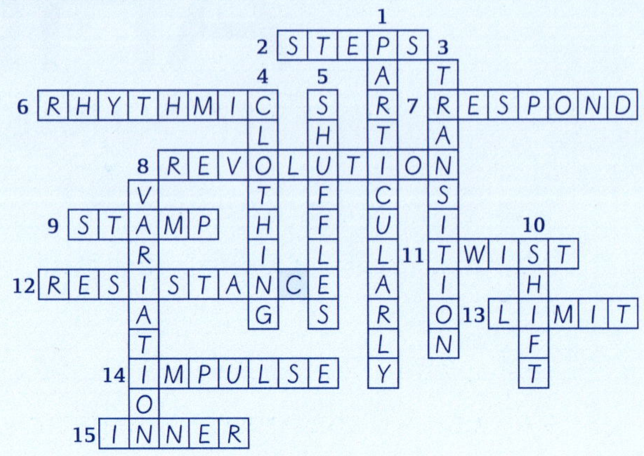

8 New words SB p. 15

1 hurry **2** era **3** Rural **4** gumboot **5** chained **6** hardship **7** slapped **8** stomped **9** Combined **10** choreographer **11** celebration

9 New words SB p. 16

a)

Solution: controversial

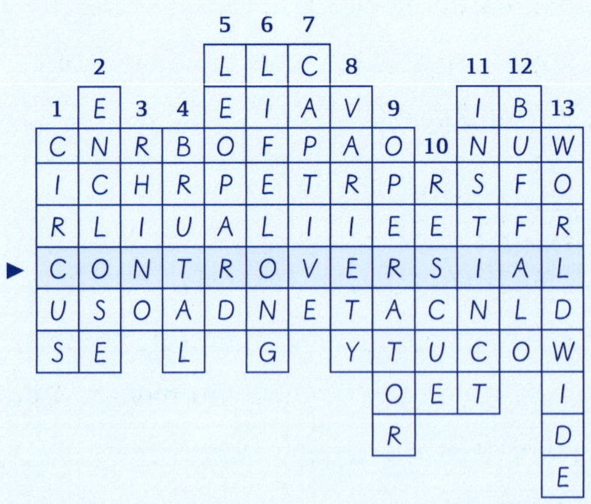

b)

1 active; radically **2** widespread; questionable **3** informative

c)

A 9 **B** 10 **C** 1 **D** 15 **E** 13 **F** 11 **G** 2 **H** 4 **I** 14 **J** 3 **K** 5 **L** 7 **M** 6 **N** 12 **O** 8

10 Antonyms

1 pessimistic **2** wrong **3** similarity
4 passive **5** fast **6** dark
7 disadvantage **8** unavailable
9 small **10** minority

11 New words SB *p. 17*

a)
1 air conditioning **2** In fact
3 circumstances **4** partial **5** refund
b)
1 complaint **2** Formulate **3** receipt
4 demand **5** consequences **6** prompts
7 elaborate **8** little

12 New words SB *p. 18*

a)
1 host **2** comedian **3** commentator
b)
A 7 **B** 10 **C** 6 **D** 12 **E** 8 **F** 13
G 1 **H** 5 **I** 9 **J** 2 **K** 3
c)
1 light-skinned **2** a leg up **3** clue
4 equated with **5** intelligence
6 get away with **7** dock **8** option
9 would yell

13 Synonyms

1 English is spoken **worldwide**.
2 Shawn has grown up in a **rural area**.
3 To get to the station you have to **take a right** at the cinema and then go straight on.
4 The Johnsons live in a **large** house.
5 Sally only watches **educational** TV programmes.

14 New words SB *p. 19*

1 serve **2** handle **3** boundary
4 versed **5** navigate **6** *across:* dude
6 *down:* shopkeeper **7** pick **8** passionate
9 confusion **10** upside **11** merely
12 oppress **13** incident **14** mug
15 brief **16** naughty **17** define
18 chameleon **19** idiot **20** perception
21 fluent

15 Verbs and nouns

2 Lots of people struggle with spelling. Some believe they have lost the struggle.
3 Lucy always counts her steps when she walks to school. Sometimes she steps into nasty things.
4 Some people don't know their limits when they drink alcohol. The law limits the alcoholic drinks that may be sold to people under 18.
5 Ahmad and Samira had to hurry to catch their bus. They were in such a hurry that they forgot their lunch boxes at home.
6 Three young people helped to rescue the lion cubs from the fire. One of them helps in a rescue centre for wild animals at the weekend.
7 Junior nurses sick animals in his free time. His two older sisters are nurses at the local hospital.
8 There has been a shift in people's attitude towards climate change. But some people try to shift people's attention away from things that need to be done about it.
9 The workers' demand for a higher pay seems reasonable. Some workers also demand higher safety standards.

16 New words SB p. 20

1 physical **2** architect **3** barriers
4 effort

17 New words SB p. 21

1 mood **2** atmosphere **3** theme

18 New words SB p. 22

1 misunderstandings **2** rephrase/clarify
3 clarify/rephrase **4** in other words
5 put

19 Synonyms

1 mostly **2** merely **3** brief
4 entrepreneur **5** youths **6** at times

My learner log

(Mögliche Lösungen)

Write three words that are often used to describe the facets of South Africa: rainbow nation, official language(s), nature reserve(s)

Write three words you need to write a film review: setting, plot, theme

2 Aotearoa – New Zealand

1 New words SB pp. 26–27

1 kiwi **2** peninsula **3** format **4** cloud
5 icon **6** Commonwealth **7** Pacific Islands
8 ethnic **9** flightless **10** sheep **11** census
12 doubtful **13** insight **14** marine

2 New words SB p. 28

a)

1 gear **2** Tackling **3** cup **4** British Isles
5 laughing their heads off **6** ritual

b)

1 integral **2** grassroots **3** mentality
4 tough **5** turning point **6** ideals **7** ties
8 psyche **9** impressive

c)

A 8 **B** 14 **C** 7 **D** 11 **E** 6 **F** 1 **G** 9
H 12 **I** 2 **J** 10 **K** 3 **L** 15 **M** 5

3 Word families: adjectives and nouns

1 cloudy – wolkig – cloud – Wolke
2 doubtful – zweifelhaft, ungewiss – doubt – Zweifel
3 important – wichtig, bedeutungsvoll – importance – Bedeutung, Wichtigkeit
4 impressive – beeindruckend – impression – Eindruck
5 intelligent – intelligent – intelligence – Intelligenz

4 New words SB p. 29

1 teammates **2** rivals **3** Union
4 sidelines **5** function **6** highly
7 powerful

5 Word families

1 characteristic **2** gatherings **3** ethnic
4 ideally

6 New words SB p. 30

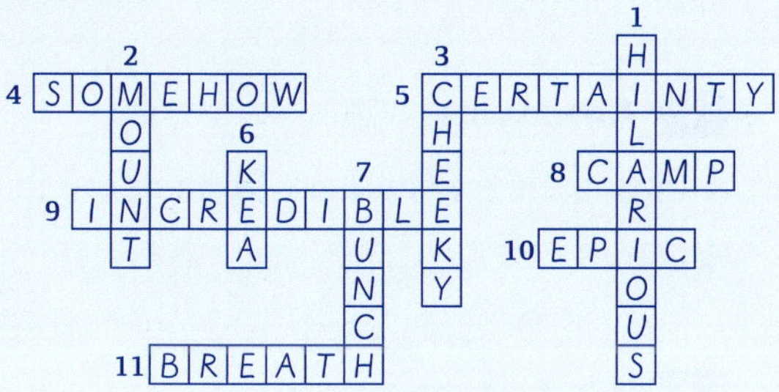

7 New words SB p. 31

1 bumped into **2** headed **3** straight
4 she has a point **5** Otherwise
6 locations **7** universe
8 spins and turns **9** absolutely

8 New words SB p. 32

a)
1 sandals **2** swimwear **3** kayak
4 campsite **5** swings **6** canyon

b)
1 guided tour **2** get informed about
3 the gist of **4** paddle **5** sunblock
6 commercial **7** strapped **8** recharge
9 Bring along

9 New words SB p. 33

A 9 **B** 7 **C** 11 **D** 2 **E** 8 **F** 1 **G** 3
H 6 **I** 4

10 Synonyms

1 rivals **2** gear **3** hilarious **4** highly
5 campground

11 New words SB p. 34

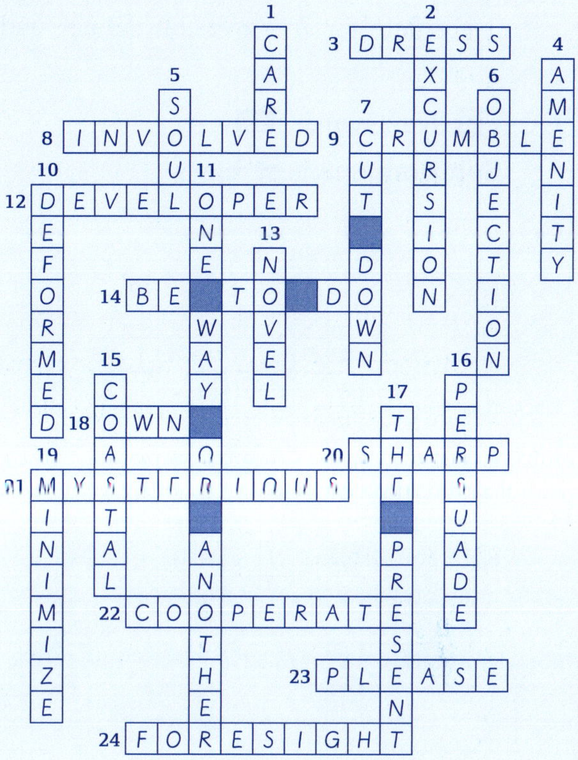

12 New words SB p. 35

a)
1 in favour of **2** craft **3** means
4 central **5** rotate **6** interest **7** cost
8 along with **9** blasted
10 lined with **11** furious
12 forehead **13** feel sorry for

b)
1 seeds **2** be seated **3** granny's
4 flames **5** dynamite

13 New words SB p. 36

A 10 **B** 12 **C** 16 **D** 14 **E** 4 **F** 5
G 13 **H** 3 **I** 15 **J** 17 **K** 6 **L** 11
M 2 **N** 8 **O** 9

14 Odd word out

1 historian **2** seed **3** importance

15 New words SB p. 37, p. 162

1 reset **2** rediscovered **3** rebuilding
4 reuse

16 Word families

1 absolutely **2** expression **3** persuade

17 New words SB *p. 38*

Solution: unacceptable

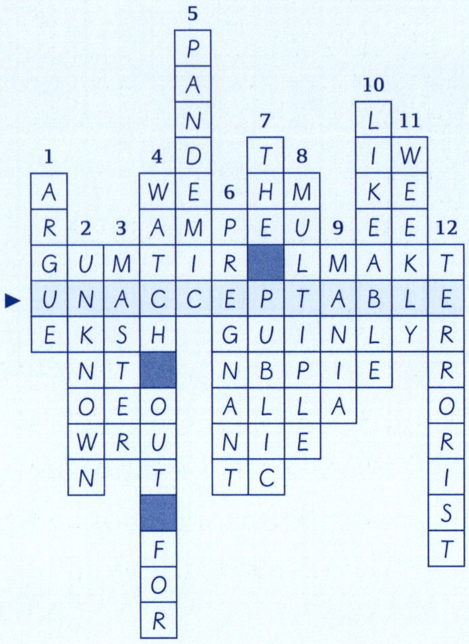

18 Key word transformation

1 Jim's parents didn't object to his plan to study abroad.

2 Laura and her parents have regular arguments about her loud music.

3 You can get / Get informed about Māori traditions on the internet.

4 Nobody knew about her pregnancy.

My learner log

(Mögliche Lösungen)

Write two examples / two Māori words: Aotearoa, Te Reo Māori, haka

Write two examples / two idioms: That's not my cup of tea. (= I don't like it very much.) Oh no! You've let the cat out of the bag. (= You've told a secret.)

Revision: Units 1 & 2

1 Antonyms

1 optimistic **2** similar **3** unacceptable **4** active

2 What are they doing?

1 stomping/stamping **2** yelling **3** serving **4** camping **5** recharging **6** strapping

3 Verbs

1 grasp **2** breed **3** Take **4** scrambled **5** persuade **6** reset

4 Adjectives

1 rural **2** lifelong **3** widespread **4** partial **5** nationwide **6** pregnant **7** multiple **8** lovely

5 Word families

1 social **2** angry **3** agreement **4** Racism **5** rhythmically **6** cooperation **7** incredibly **8** care

3 Into the world

1 New words SB pp. 42–43

1 gap **2** managed **3** term **4** budgeting **5** overspend **6** make up my mind **7** Yippee **8** I can't wait **9** run out of money **10** au pair **11** tidying up **12** ironing **13** heating **14** placemats

2 New words SB p. 44

a)

A 10 **B** 7 **C** 1 **D** 8 **E** 3 **F** 4 **G** 5 **H** 2 **I** 11

b)

1 backgrounds **2** meet **3** disadvantaged **4** hands-on **5** in order to

c)

Solution: construction

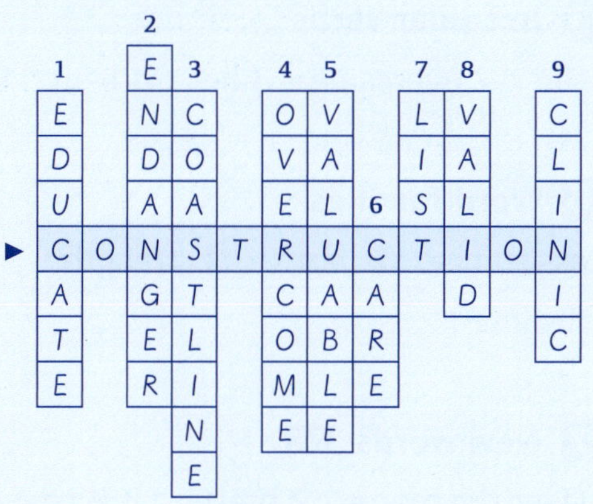

3 New words SB p. 45

1 is located in **2** served **3** ecological **4** Besides **5** preparation **6** understandable **7** are prepared **8** mistake

4 New words SB p. 46

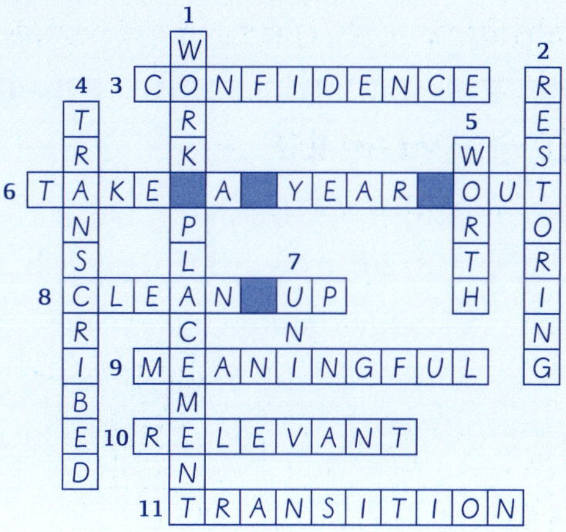

5 Synonyms

work placement – internship, (to) make a decision – (to) make up your mind, (to) make sb./sth. stronger – (to) strengthen sb./sth., (to) be prepared to do sth. – (to) be ready to do sth., essential – very important

6 New words SB p. 47

A 7 **B** 9 **C** 1 **D** 3 **E** 8 **F** 4 **G** 6

7 Phrasal verbs

1 out **2** on **3** up **4** on **5** up **6** into **7** along

8 New words SB p. 48

1 dormitory **2** laneways **3** double room **4** en suite **5** stocked **6** common room **7** pool **8** store **9** blocks **10** note

9 New words SB p. 49

a)

1 literally **2** expectation **3** agency **4** considered **5** depend on **6** additional **7** on bad terms **8** accept **9** take advantage of **10** trade-off **11** on a par

b)

1 ... gave the police a **precise** description ...
2 ... buy a **return** ticket.
3 **Housecleaning** can be fun ...
4 ... work **up to** 45 hours per week.

10 New words SB p. 50

a)

A 9 **B** 6 **C** 7 **D** 11 **E** 10 **F** 8 **G** 2
H 1 **I** 4 **J** 5 **K** 3

b)

1 No idea. **2** narrow **3** (to) give sb. a hand **4** (to) go round **5** (to) slide

c)

11
1 WHEEL
2 LOVING
3 STARTLE
4 WAREHOUSE
5 SOUR
6 SLIGHT
7 CLIPBOARD
8 DAMN
9 LOGISTICS
10 SLUMP

11 Word families

1 heating **2** endangered **3** educational
4 confidence

12 New words SB p. 51

a)

1 Shall I **2** anecdotes **3** sheepish
4 accommodate **5** making such a fuss
6 shipped **7** distant **8** fell over

b)

A 8 **B** 6 **C** 10 **D** 1 **E** 9 **F** 2 **G** 5
H 4 **I** 7

c)

9
1 EXTEND
2 STRAIGHTEN
3 MANOEUVRE
4 DEGREE
5 GLOW
6 SHOVE
7 SURF
8 SHUFFLE

13 Verbs and nouns

1 I always listen to music when I iron my shirts. My neighbour borrowed my iron last night.
2 Sam's budget is really low, but he learned to budget from his parents.
3 When our house was broken into, we had to make a list of everything that was missing. Now I immediately list things when I buy them.
4 In order to slow down climate change countries need to transition from fossil fuels to renewable energy. This transition will not be easy.
5 Some of the sports exercises were really hard. Leila exercises three hours every day.

14 Antonyms

1 irrelevant **2** return **3** narrow **4** budget

15 Irregular verbs

1 slid **2** overcame **3** bet **4** bent **5** bred

16 Word families

1 assistance **2** partly **3** strength
4 distant

17 New words SB p. 52

1 Over the moon **2** pretty **3** It pays to
4 nerds **5** grinning **6** poke
7 work out **8** get a taste **9** speculating
10 There you go **11** let out a sigh
12 flat **13** sink **14** outcome
15 get lucky **16** Yep **17** idiomatic

18 New words SB p. 53–54

A 9 **B** 6 **C** 7 **D** 8 **E** 2 **F** 1 **G** 5
H 4 **I** 3

19 Compounds

1 au pair **2** housecleaning **3** gap year
4 clipboard **5** placemat **6** coastline
7 safety vest **8** laneway **9** warehouse
10 double room **11** work placement
12 hard hat

20 Word building

1 endless **2** sleepless **3** timeless
4 useless / hopeless **5** hopeless / useless
6 homeless

My learner log

(Mögliche Lösungen)
Write three words for two different word families: strength – strong – strengthen; danger – dangerous – endanger
Write five such words / words that end in "-less": boneless, flightless, helpless, jobless, thoughtless

4 The future in our hands

1 New words SB *pp. 58–59*

1 donation **2** individual **3** extinction
4 (to) participate (in) **5** (to) cycle
6 consumerism **7** (to) examine

2 New words SB *p. 60*

a)
A 7 **B** 5 **C** 9 **D** 3 **E** 4 **F** 1 **G** 6
b)
1 no longer **2** ends up **3** harmony
4 front line **5** toxic **6** first-hand
7 marginalize
c)

				7					
				L					
		1	M	A	J	O	R		
		2	U	N	I	T	E	D	
			3	D	A	M	A	G	E
4	C	R	I	S	I	S			
				L					
5	A	C	T	I	V	I	S	M	
				D					
	6	F	R	E	Q	U	E	N	T

3 New words SB *p. 61*

1 inseparable **2** floodwaters **3** at risk
4 solidarity **5** tackle **6** related
7 unjustly **8** targeted **9** counterparts
10 exaggerated

4 New words SB *p. 62*

a)
1 cutlery **2** committee **3** reusable
4 average **5** biodegradable
6 containers **7** enables **8** General Assembly
b)
1 intention **2** intercultural **3** approve
4 till **5** capable of **6** adapted
7 innovation **8** bringing up
9 commitments

5 (to) relate – related – relation – relationship

1 related **2** relationship **3** relation
4 related **5** related **6** relation
7 relates **8** relate **9** relationship

6 Word families

1 examinations/exams **2** donations
3 activist **4** frequency **5** containers

7 New words SB p. 63

1 planet **2** amount; carbon dioxide
3 leadership **4** measures; transform
5 comparison **6** open-minded

8 New words SB p. 64

A 6 **B** 7 **C** 2 **D** 3 **E** 4 **F** 5

9 Verbs and nouns

1 It's horrible to witness a crime. If you are invited as a witness, the police are interested in everything you heard or saw.
2 A storm caused huge damage to the church. The roof needs to be repaired immediately. Otherwise, rain will damage the paintings inside the church.
3 The club wants to reach its target of 100 new members by the end of the year. A newly offered course will target young people who love dancing.
4 Police officers sometimes risk their life to save other people. Not everyone wants to take that risk.
5 The Millers' new swimming pool measures 8 metres long and 3 metres wide. Their neighbours hope that they will take measures to prevent children and animals from falling into it.

10 New words SB p. 65

1 balance **2** rather **3** evidence
4 journalism **5** spot on **6** expose
7 once more **8** what's more **9** punished
10 representative **11** criminal
12 praise
Solution: letter to the editor

11 New words SB p. 66

a)
1 is stroking **2** is tugging **3** is rushing
4 is squeezing **5** is balling **6** is typing
b)
1 crook **2** Flash freezing **3** colony
4 laboratory **5** anything but **6** cram
7 approached
c)
A 6 **B** 9 **C** 8 **D** 11 **E** 2 **F** 12 **G** 3
H 10 **I** 4 **J** 5 **K** 7 **L** 1
d)
1 liquid **2** wire **3** vein **4** lid **5** chest
6 bubbles **7** muscle **8** tube **9** shoebox
10 hose

12 New words SB p. 67

a)
1 jerked **2** stuck **3** For Pete's sake!
4 point **5** backing down **6** guilted
7 crops **8** insides **9** trails **10** slammed
11 intravenous **12** needle
b)
A 6 **B** 8 **C** 12 **D** 2 **E** 9 **F** 10 **G** 13
H 11 **I** 5 **J** 4 **K** 1 **L** 3 **M** 7

13 Antonyms

1 (to) undress **2** uninhabitable
3 unjust **4** balanced **5** narrow-minded

14 Word families

1 lowered **2** criminal **3** reusable
4 leader

15 New words SB p. 68

1 translucent **2** solid **3** watery
4 goes under **5** splutter **6** drifts

16 New words SB p. 69

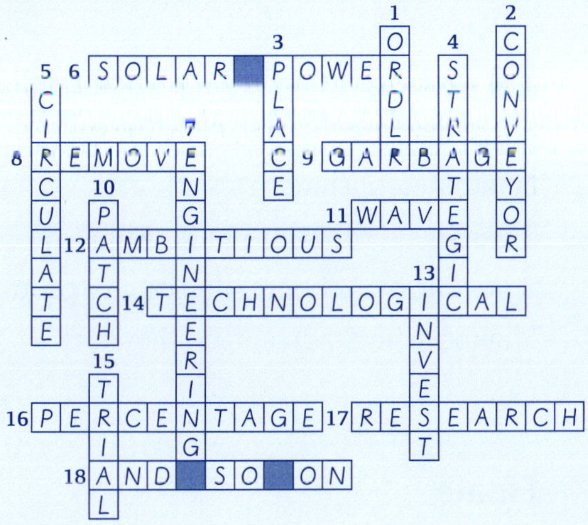

17 Synonyms

1 Aisha **no longer works** here.

2 Mia doesn't like **participating** in discussions.

3 Sam always **cycles** to work.

4 Liam's broken leg is **very painful**.

5 Jake plays **a major** role in the school play.

18 Word families: adjectives and nouns

1 extinct – ausgestorben – extinction – Ausrottung, Aussterben

2 intentional – absichtlich, beabsichtigt – intention – Absicht, Vorsatz

3 just – gerecht – justice – Gerechtigkeit

19 New words SB p. 70

1 has expanded **2** systematic
3 grouped **4** contribute **5** so far

20 Verbs and prepositions

1 on **2** for **3** up **4** away **5** into
6 in **7** to **8** down

My learner log

(Mögliche Lösungen)

Write two examples of expressing your opinion in a letter or email: I don't see it that way.
I couldn't agree more.

Write two examples of environmental action:
take part in climate action, recycle things

Revision: Units 3 & 4

1 What are they doing?

1 is tidying (up) **2** is examining
3 are cleaning up **4** is wrapping; around
5 is ironing **6** is renovating

2 Adjectives

1 precise **2** frequent **3** solid
4 essential **5** valid **6** ambitious
7 disadvantaged

3 What are the people saying?

1 Yippee! **2** It's not rocket science.
3 There you go! **4** I took it by mistake.
5 I've got it. **6** Damn!

4 Word families

1 confidence **2** storage **3** adaptable
4 investment **5** heating

5 Synonyms

a)
(to) change sth. completely – (to) transform, (to) produce (goods) – (to) manufacture, eco-friendly – environmentally friendly, strategy – tactic, (to) tug – (to) pull, rather – quite, meaningful – serious, weird – strange, piece of clothing – garment

b)
2 produce / manufacture things ...
eco-friendly / environmentally friendly
3 strategy / tactic
4 a rather weird / quite a weird / a rather strange / quite a strange situation
5 tugging / pulling him
6 meaningful / serious job. ... pieces of clothing / garments

6 American English – British English

1 (to) maneuver – (to) manoeuvre – manövrieren, steuern
2 garbage – rubbish – Müll, Abfall
3 downtown London – in the city centre of London – im Stadtzentrum Londons

Finale

1 A crossword puzzle

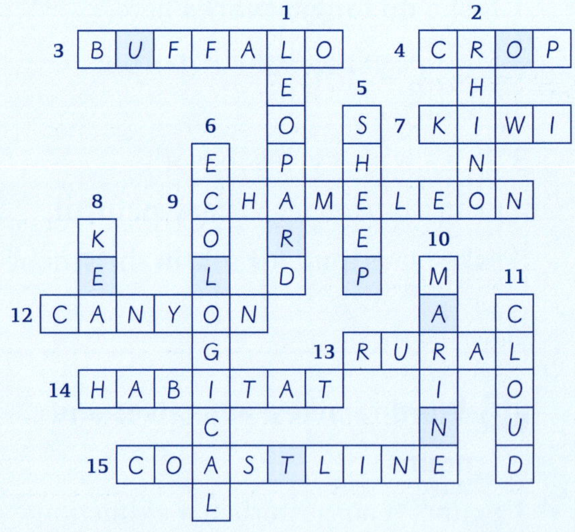

Solution: our planet

2 The big Go Ahead quiz

GREAT JOB, WORDMASTER!

c) Write the missing words in the crossword. The letters in the blue boxes form a word that you use when you talk about the building of something, especially roads, houses, bridges, etc. You need to add a few letters to complete the word.

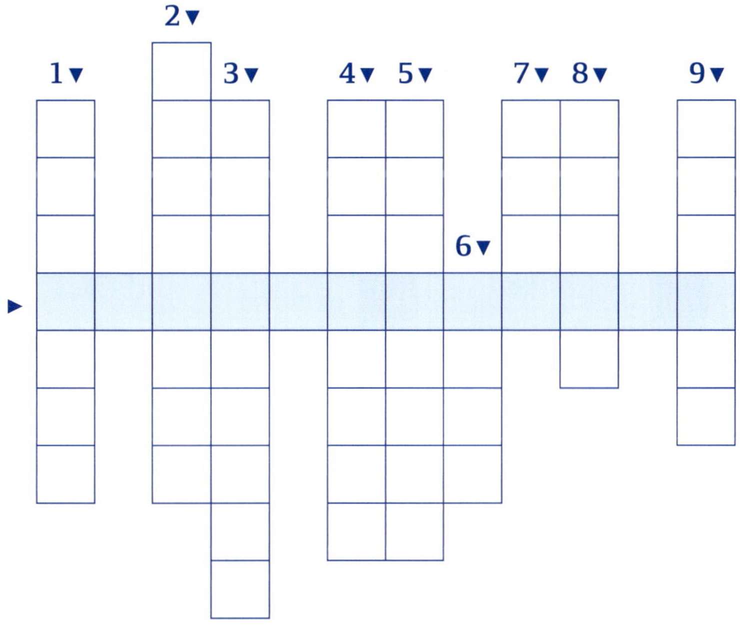

1 (to) teach sb. for a certain time at school or university
2 (to) put sb. or sth. in a situation in which they can be hurt or damaged
3 the land along a coast
4 (to) solve a problem
5 having a high value
6 providing things sb. needs for their health or protection
7 (to) write things down in a particular order
8 legally acceptable
9 a place where you can go for special medical treatment or advice

3 New words SB p. 45

Read the sentences and complete them with a word from the box.

is located in • are prepared • besides • ecological • mistake • preparation • served • understandable

Our hotel **1** ______________ a small village by the sea. Breakfast is **2** ______________ from 8 am till 11 am. Our **3** ______________ standards are very high. **4** ______________ buying our food locally, we avoid plastic and save on water and electricity. We run cooking classes for children and let them help with the **5** ______________ of meals if they wish. Allergies are becoming a problem for a growing number of people, and it's perfectly **6** ______________ that they want to feel safe on holiday. Our staff **7** ______________ to listen to all our guests' needs. Help us to improve our service: Inform us about any **8** ______________ we make!

4 New words SB p. 46

Write the missing words in the crossword.

2 Jay is ??? an old wardrobe.

5 This house is ??? a million pounds.

1 If you're not sure what job would suit you, do a ??? ??? to find out.
3 Luana's parents have always had a lot of ??? in their daughter's abilities.
4 Reece recorded the interview and then ??? it.
6 Philip and Paul want to ??? ??? ??? ??? after their final exams.
7 After that they're planning to go to ???.
8 Will you please ??? ??? after using the kitchen!
9 Most people want to do ??? work.
10 If you apply for a job, ??? work experience will help you to get it.
11 Lots of companies have not yet completed the ??? to the digital world.

5 Synonyms

Match the expressions that have a similar meaning. Draw lines.

work placement
(to) be prepared to do sth.
very important
(to) make a decision
(to) be ready to do sth.
(to) strengthen sb./sth.
(to) make sb./sth. stronger
internship
essential
(to) make up your mind

6 New words SB p. 47

Match the words (A–G) with the corresponding definitions (1–9). Write the correct numbers in the grid below. Be careful: There are two definitions that you don't need.

A down under
B gardener
C on offer
D resort
E … though.
F trek
G visa

1 that can be bought, hired, rented, etc.
2 ►► far away
3 a popular place where people go on holiday
4 a long walk; a long riding trip
5 what you can see from a particular point
6 a stamp put in your passport that gives you permission to enter a foreign country
7 an informal expression for Australia and New Zealand
8 an adverb used to make the previous statement less important
9 a person whose job is to look after plants, water flowers and cut the grass

A	B	C	D	E	F	G

7 Phrasal verbs

Complete the sentences with the right preposition.

along • into • on (2x) • out • up (2x)

1 Joel and his friends returned home from their trip when they ran ______________ of money.
2 Samira and her friend want to go on holiday together. They haven't agreed ______________ where to go yet.
3 Martha often finds it hard to make ______________ her mind about what she wants to eat.
4 Social media caught ______________ with young people very quickly.
5 Norah tidies ______________ her room once a week. She's a very well-organized person.
6 Lea hadn't seen Daniel for five years before she bumped ______________ him last Monday.
7 The party starts at 8 pm. Everybody should bring ______________ something to eat.

8 New words SB p. 48

Read what Kyong tells his friend Sam about his visit to Melbourne. Complete the sentences with the words from the box.

blocks • common room • dormitory • double room • en suite • laneways • note • pool • stocked • store

Hi Sam, greetings from Melbourne. Kim and I arrived here last night and were lucky to find beds in a hostel. The city is full of backpackers. There are young people from all over the world! We're sharing a **1** ______________ with nine other people, but it's fine. The hostel is in one of Melbourne's cute **2** ______________. Not all of them are cute though. Some are quite dirty with walls full of graffiti. But there are cafes and restaurants in ours. So that's really nice.

We would have preferred a **3** ______________ in a hotel but didn't find a reasonably priced one. Kim would have liked an **4** ______________ bathroom. On the other hand, the hostel has a fully **5** ______________ kitchen and a comfortable **6** ______________ where we played **7** ______________ with two Japanese guys last night. We can **8** ______________ our luggage here when we go sightseeing, and there are lots of interesting museums and other sights just a few **9** ______________ from here. Please **10** ______________ that we might be offline next week when we go hiking in Werribee Gorge.

Bye for now and say hello to Kira from me

Kyong

9 New words SB p. 49

a) Read the sentences and circle the right words.

1 The word "safari" literally / additionally means "journey".

2 The agency / expectation is that she will get the job.

3 Emma found her job through an expectation / agency.

4 Tom never considered / was on a par with working abroad.

5 Children depend on / trade-off their parents.

6 The hotel provides trade-off / additional blankets when required.

7 Most people hate to be on bad terms / on a par with their neighbours.

8 Please take advantage of / accept my apology for being late.

9 Criminals take advantage of / trade-off unsafe passwords.

10 Three weeks paid holiday in exchange for six months work is a fair trade-off / agency.

11 Our hotel is on friendly terms / on a par with other excellent hotels in town.

b) Rewrite each sentence with the right opposite (◄►) or synonym (►►) from the box.

housecleaning • precise • return • up to

1 Harry gave the police an exact description of the people who stole his bike.

►► ______________________________

2 If you want to come back the same day, buy a single ticket.

◄► ______________________________

3 Cleaning the house can be fun if all the family take part in it.

►► ______________________________

4 Au pairs will have to work no more than 45 hours per week.

►► ______________________________

10 New words SB p. 50

a) What do the following words mean? Match the expressions (A–K) with their corresponding definitions (1–11). Write the correct numbers in the grid below.

A (to) bet
B (to) boom
C dodo
D enthusiastic
E hard hat
F hard-working
G It's not rocket science.
H safety vest
I She's worth her weight in gold.
J (to) skip
K (to) walk sb. somewhere

1 sth. bright yellow or orange you wear over your normal clothes so that people can see you well
2 *You say this to express that you are not impressed by sb.'s achievement.*
3 (to) go somewhere with somebody in order to make sure that the person gets there safely
4 *You say this to express that sb. is valuable or does her job very well.*
5 not to do sth. that you should normally do
6 (to) make a very loud and deep sound
7 a bird that died out centuries ago
8 putting a lot of effort into a job
9 *You use this word to say that you are almost certain that sth. is true or that sth. will happen.*
10 sth. building workers, etc. wear to protect their heads
11 showing a lot of interest or excitement about sb. or sth.

A	B	C	D	E	F	G	H	I	J	K

b) Find the right opposites (◄►) or synonyms (►►).

(to) slide • narrow • (to) go round • No idea. • (to) give sb. a hand

1 Not a clue. ►► ____________________
2 wide ◄► ____________________
3 (to) help sb. ►► ____________________
4 (to) rotate ►► ____________________
5 (to) stand still ◄► ____________________

c) Write the missing words in the crossword. The letters in the blue boxes form the word for number **11**.

7

1 (to) push or pull sth. that has wheels
2 feeling or showing love for sb. or sth.
3 (to) frighten or shock sb. with a sudden or unexpected action
4 a building where goods are stored before they are brought to shops to be sold
5 the taste of lemons
6 very small in degree
8 *an exclamation that you use when you are angry, annoyed or disappointed about yourself*
9 the organization that is needed to make a company work successfully
10 (to) sit down heavily
11 a strong feeling of interest or excitement in sth.

11 Word families

Use the word given in capitals at the end of each line to form another word of the same word family that fits in the sentence.

1 "It's very cold today. Let's put the ______________ on."	**HEAT**
2 We must protect ______________ animals and plants.	**DANGER**
3 Some TV stations offer good ______________ programmes.	**EDUCATE**
4 Lara gained a lot of ______________ during her internship.	**CONFIDENT**

12 New words SB p. 51

a) Read the sentences and complete them with a word from the box.

accommodate • anecdotes • distant • fell over • making such a fuss • shall I • sheepish • shipped

1 "It's very hot in here." – "________________ open the window?"

2 When we were kids, Dad used to tell us lots of ________________ from his past.

3 I can tell from the ________________ look on your face that something is wrong.

4 The Millers have a big house. They can easily ________________ 20 guests.

5 "It's just a small hole in your jeans. Stop ________________ about it!"

6 Lots of goods are ________________ into the EU every year.

7 We heard the ________________ sound of an engine but couldn't see a car.

8 Tim tripped over his own feet and ________________.

b) What do the following words mean? Match the expressions (A–I) with their corresponding definitions (1–11). Write the correct numbers in the grid below. Be careful: There are two definitions that you don't need.

	1 (to) put your arms around sb. and hold them tight
A downtown …	2 a particular position in which sb. sits or stands
B exercise	3 ►► bright
C honey	4 having an attractive shape *(said for example of a car or a boat)*
D (to) hug (sb.)	5 ►► quiet
E I've got it.	6 movement / sport activity
F pose	7 ►► strange
G silent	8 ►► (in) the centre of …
H sleek	9 ►► It's OK, I can manage.
I weird	10 a name some people call someone they love
	11 ◄► message

A	B	C	D	E	F	G	H	I

*c) Write the missing words in the crossword. The letters in the blue boxes form the word for number **9**.*

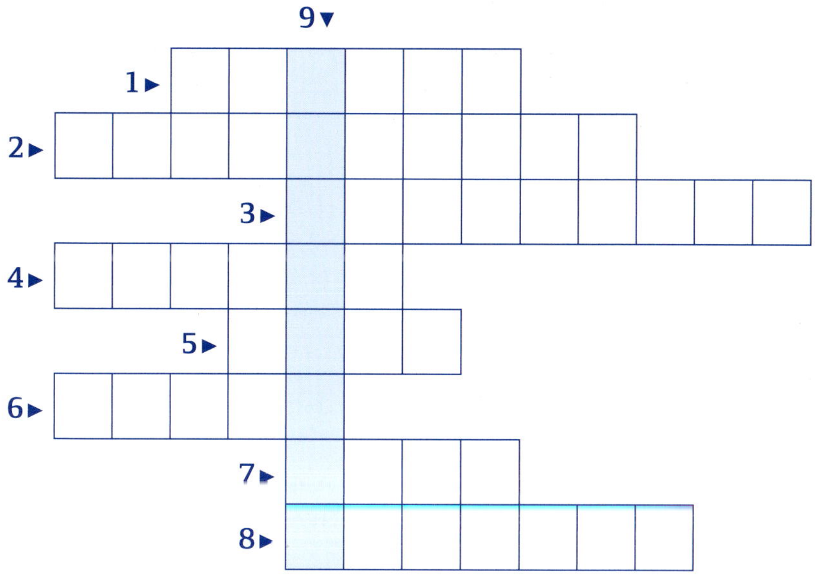

1 (to) make sth. longer or wider
2 (to) become or make sth. straight
3 (to) move sth. with care
4 the qualification that students get when they successfully complete a university course
5 the light from a fire
6 (to) push sb. or sth.
7 what waves in the sea produce when they crash onto the beach or onto rocks
8 (to) move sth. into a different position
9 existing forever

13 Verbs and nouns

Read the sentences. Some verbs and nouns look the same. Circle the nouns and underline the verbs.

1 I always listen to music when I iron my shirts.
My neighbour borrowed my iron last night.

2 Sam's budget is really low, but he learned to budget from his parents.

3 When our house was broken into, we had to make a list of everything that was missing. Now I immediately list things when I buy them.

4 In order to slow down climate change countries need to transition from fossil fuels[1] to renewable energy. This transition will not be easy.

5 Some of the sports exercises were really hard. Leila exercises three hours every day.

[1] fossil fuels ['fɒsl 'fjuːəls] *fossile Brennstoffe*

14 Antonyms

Find a word that has the opposite meaning of the underlined word.

1 Fill in the form with relevant information about yourself. ______________________

2 How much is a one-way ticket to London? ______________________

3 A wide road led down to the beach. ______________________

4 Young people have to learn to overspend. ______________________

15 Irregular verbs

Read the sentences and complete them with a verb from the box. Be careful about the tense.

bend • bet • breed • overcome • slide

1 Their car ______________________ down the icy road and crashed into a road sign.

2 Daniel ______________________ his fear and jumped into the swimming pool.

3 I'll ______________________ you can't run faster than me.

4 He ______________________ down and picked up the broken plate from the floor.

5 Siobhan's grandparents ______________________ Irish sheep dogs in the past.

16 Word families

Use the word given in capitals at the end of each line to form a word of the same word family that fits in the sentence.

1 "Please inform our staff if you need ______________________."	ASSIST
2 The rising costs of living are ______________________ due to the risen costs of energy.	PART
3 It takes a long time to build up physical ______________________ again after a serious illness.	STRONG
4 Sam got an email from a ______________________ uncle he didn't know.	DISTANCE

17 New words SB p. 52

Complete the dialogue with the words from the box.

flat • get a taste • get lucky • grinning • idiomatic • it pays to • let out a sigh • over the moon • nerds • outcome • poke • pretty • sink • speculating • there you go • work out • yep

Cem: Hi, Zoe, how are you?

Zoe: **1** ______________________, Cem, to be honest. I've been accepted at Oxford University!

Cem: Congratulations, Zoe! That's **2** ______________________ cool. Well, as my mum always says: **3** ______________________ work hard at school! I hope you don't become one of those IT **4** ______________________ though ☺.

Zoe: Stop **5** ______________________, or I'll **6** ______________________ you.

Cem: Come on, I'm only joking. I'm sure things will **7** ______________________ fine for you.

Zoe: Mum and I are going to Oxford next week so that I can **8** ______________________ of the city and see if I think I can live there.

Cem: Oh Zoe, stop **9** ______________________. You'll manage!

Zoe: That's what my parents say too.

Cem: **10** ______________________.

Zoe: Well, I wonder if Mum is honest with me. She **11** ______________________ when I opened the letter and told her I got accepted. She congratulated me with quite a **12** ______________________ voice.

Cem: Well, she didn't **13** ______________________ to the ground and cry, did she?

Zoe: Could you be serious for once! No, she didn't. What about you then?

Cem: Well, I'm not sure yet what I want to do, so I've applied for a few internships. I don't know what the **14** ______________________ is yet, but if I **15** ______________________, I might be placed in an expensive restaurant by the sea.

Zoe: So you're still thinking about becoming a cook?

Cem: **16** ______________________, although the **17** ______________________ job title is "chef".

18 New words SB pp. 53–54

What do the following words mean? Match the expressions (A–I) with their corresponding definitions (1–9). Write the correct numbers in the grid below.

A either
B (to) interact
C memory
D possibility
E (to) quit
F reminder
G (to) shop for sth.
H sooner or later
I summary

1 sth. that makes you think about or remember sth.
2 ►► (to) stop
3 a short text that contains only the main points of sth.
4 at some time in the future
5 ►► (to) buy things
6 ►► (to) communicate
7 the ability to remember things
8 ►► option
9 one or the other of two

A	B	C	D	E	F	G	H	I

19 Compounds

Match the words to form compounds. Write them down. Be careful: Some compounds are written in one word, others are written in two words.

au vest hard cleaning
house safety pair hat
gap lane mat line
clip double house placement
place ware board year
coast work way room

1 ______________________ 7 ______________________
2 ______________________ 8 ______________________
3 ______________________ 9 ______________________
4 ______________________ 10 ______________________
5 ______________________ 11 ______________________
6 ______________________ 12 ______________________

20 Word building

Add "-less" to the words from the box and complete the sentences with the new words.

end • home • hope • sleep • time • use

1 The game will never be boring as there are ____________ variations one can play.

2 They were so worried about their son that they spent lots of ____________ nights.

3 Most houses in Venice are of ____________ beauty.

4 If people don't believe in science, it's ____________ trying to convince them.

5 Asking for a pay rise was ____________ as the company's situation was bad.

6 Community centres often offer help for the ____________.

My learner log

Mein Lerntagebuch. Hier notierst du deine Erfahrungen mit dem Wörterlernen.

★ My three favourite words in this unit are:

____

I can …

- remember more new English words by learning different words of the same word family. *(Write three words for two different word families.)*

____

____

- build new words by adding "-less" to nouns. *(Write five such words.)*

____

____

What was difficult in Unit 3:

____

What was easy in Unit 3:

____

What I liked about Unit 3:

____

Unit 4

The future in our hands

1 New words SB pp. 58–59

Read the definitions and write the words from the box next to them.

consumerism • (to) cycle • donation • (to) examine • extinction • individual • (to) participate (in)

1 sth. you give to a person or a charity in order to help them: ______

2 a single person: ______

3 the fact that a plant or an animal dies out for ever: ______

4 ►► (to) take part (in): ______

5 ►► (to) ride a bike: ______

6 the buying and using of lots of goods: ______

7 (to) study a thing, an animal or a person very carefully: ______

2 New words SB p. 60

a) What do the following words mean? Match the expressions (A–G) with the corresponding definitions (1–9). Be careful: There are two definitions that you don't need.

A dump
B elderly
C habitable
D impact
E intense
F painful
G (to) witness sth.

1 hurting very much
2 ◄► expensive
3 the effect that sth. has on sb. or sth.
4 ►► very great or strong
5 a more polite word for "old"
6 (to) see sth. such as an accident or a crime
7 a place where waste is taken
8 ►► stupid
9 suitable for people to live in

A	B	C	D	E	F	G

b) Complete the sentences with the right word or expression from the box.

ends up • first-hand • front line • harmony • marginalize • no longer • toxic

1 There used to be a bus service that connected the village with the train station, but it ________________ exists.

2 A lot of people buy more food than they can eat so that it ________________ in the bin.

3 Many young people wish to live in ________________ with nature.

4 Teachers feel they are on the ________________ every day, teaching children and talking to parents who aren't always happy with what's going on at school.

5 Activists have been fighting against ________________ waste being dumped in rivers and oceans for years.

6 People in Christchurch, New Zealand, witnessed ________________ the damage the 2011 earthquake did to their city.

7 Politicians need to make sure that their decisions don't ________________ any group of society.

*c) Write the missing words in the crossword. The letters in the blue boxes form the word for number **7**. You have to add a few letters to complete the word.*

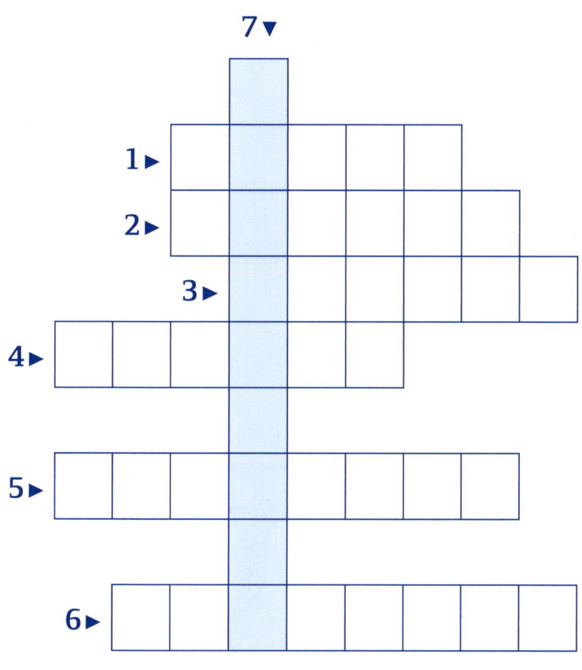

1 ►► very large, very important

2 West and East Germany ??? again in 1989 and signed a contract in 1990.

3 Floods, storms and fires do a lot of ??? to the environment.

4 a time of great danger and difficulty where important decisions must be made

5 the activity of working to achieve political or social change

6 ►► very often

7 

3 New words SB p. 61

Complete the sentences with the words from the box.

counterparts • exaggerated • floodwaters • inseparable • related • at risk • solidarity • tackle • targeted • unjustly

Alfie and his dog are **1** ______________________. When the **2** ______________________ reached Alfie's house, his dog realized that they were both **3** ______________________ of drowning. He barked and woke Alfie and together they climbed on the roof and were rescued.

The villagers experienced a lot of **4** ______________________ after the floods had destroyed their houses. Strangers came to help them **5** ______________________ the problems they now had. Everybody agreed that the heavy rainfall was **6** climate- ______________________ and demanded immediate action from local politicians. But they felt **7** ______________________ **8** ______________________.

Later that day local news reporters and their national **9** ______________________ said in television interviews that the villagers' demand for help wasn't **10** ______________________ at all.

4 New words SB p. 62

a) Complete the sentences with the correct words from the box. Use the pictures to help you.

average • biodegradable • committee • containers • cutlery • enables • General Assembly • reusable

1 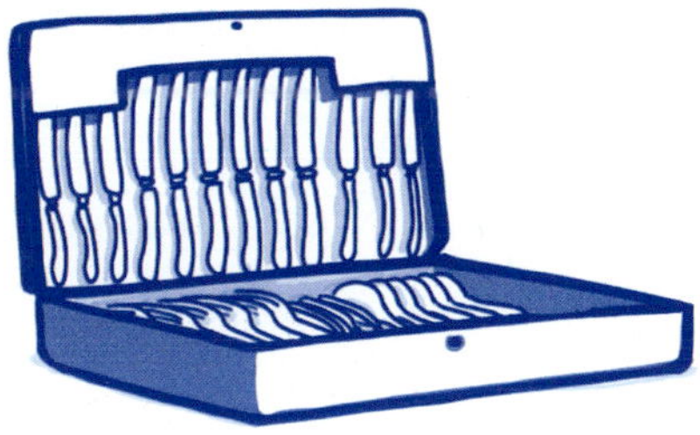

"We got a ______________ set for our wedding."

2 

The ______________ meeting lasted till midnight.

3 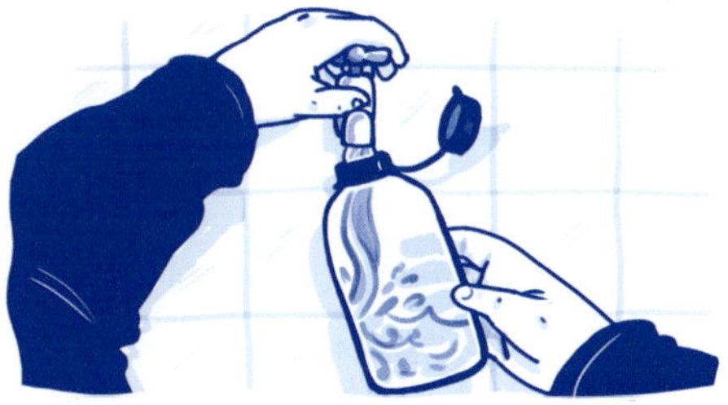

Hostels appreciate it if their guests bring a ______________ bottle.

4 

The ______________ age of our participants is 13 years.

5 

All our products are plastic-free and ______________.

6 

"We try to avoid waste. Please bring your own ______________."

7 

"My electric wheelchair ______________ me to lead a very independent life."

8 

All 193 members of the United Nations are also members of the ______________.

b) Read the sentences and circle the right words.

1 Please accept my apologies: It wasn't my intention / innovation to frighten you.

2 Young people profit a lot from innovation / intercultural exchanges.

3 Jim wanted to leave school at 15, but his parents didn't approve / adapt.

4 Lea had never considered working abroad unless / till she met a group of young architects who convinced her that working abroad was very exciting.

5 It's amazing what children are capable of / approve of when they are taught by inspiring teachers.

6 Kaya grew up in a small village, but she adapted / approved very quickly to her new life in the city when she started her first job in Johannesburg.

7 Scientists agree that we need more technological intention / innovation to produce enough sustainable energy for the world population.

8 Jim knew that his parents didn't want him to leave school at 15, but he kept approving / bringing up the subject over and over again.

9 If we want to reduce global warming, everybody has to make commitments / intentions.

5 (to) relate – related – relation – relationship

Complete the sentences with the right word from the box. You can use some of the words more than once.

relate • related • relates • relation • relationship

1 We carry the same surname but we are not ____________________.

2 How would you describe the ____________________ between you and your sister?

3 Australia is a huge country in ____________________ to its population.

4 His bad mood is probably ____________________ to the fact that he lost his job.

5 Most of Sarah's problems are health- ____________________.

6 Describe the ____________________ between the text and the photos.

7 The book that has just been published ____________________ to poverty in Ireland in the 19th century.

8 How does the report ____________________ to your own experience?

9 I never really understood my grandparents' ____________________. They hardly ever talked to each other.

6 Word families

Use the word given in capitals at the end of each line to form another word of the same word family that fits in the sentence.

1 The students will take four ________________ in June.	EXAMINE
2 Many charities depend on ________________.	DONATE
3 Leroy became an environmental ________________ when he was 15.	ACTIVISM
4 Storms are hitting tropical islands with increasing ________________.	FREQUENT
5 Shops should sell more goods in reusable ________________.	CONTAIN

7 New words SB p. 63

Complete the sentences with the words from the box.

amount • carbon dioxide • comparison • leadership • measures • open-minded • planet • transform

1 We need to protect our ________________ Earth.

2 Scientists agree that we need to reduce the ________________ of ________________ that we put in the air.

3 Activists demand that industrial countries take a ________________ role in producing and using sustainable energy.

4 Some countries have already started to take ________________ to ________________ the energy sector.

5 But the production of green energy is still too low in ________________ with the energy that is gained from non-renewable sources such as oil and gas.

6 Politicians need to be more ________________ towards necessary changes.

8 New words SB p. 64

What do the following words mean? Match the expressions (A–F) with the corresponding definitions (1–8). Be careful: There are two definitions that you don't need.

A eco-friendly
B garment
C (to) investigate
D (to) manufacture
E presenter
F (to) uncover

1 a piece of decoration
2 (to) examine carefully
3 (to) produce large numbers/amounts of goods
4 ►► host
5 (to) find out sth. that was hidden or secret
6 not harming the environment
7 a piece of clothing
8 (to) put money in a bank

A	B	C	D	E	F

9 Verbs and nouns

Read the sentences. Some verbs and nouns look the same. Circle the nouns and underline the verbs.

1. It's horrible to witness a crime. If you are invited as a witness, the police are interested in everything you heard or saw.
2. A storm caused huge damage to the church. The roof needs to be repaired immediately. Otherwise, rain will damage the paintings inside the church.
3. The club wants to reach its target of 100 new members by the end of the year. A newly offered course will target young people who love dancing.
4. Police officers sometimes risk their life to save other people. Not everyone wants to take that risk.
5. The Millers' new swimming pool measures 8 metres long and 3 metres wide. Their neighbours hope that they will take measures to prevent children and animals from falling into it.

10 New words SB p. 65

Write the missing words in the crossword. The letters in the blue boxes form the expression for something you write and send to a newspaper or magazine to express your opinion. You have to add a few letters to complete the expression.

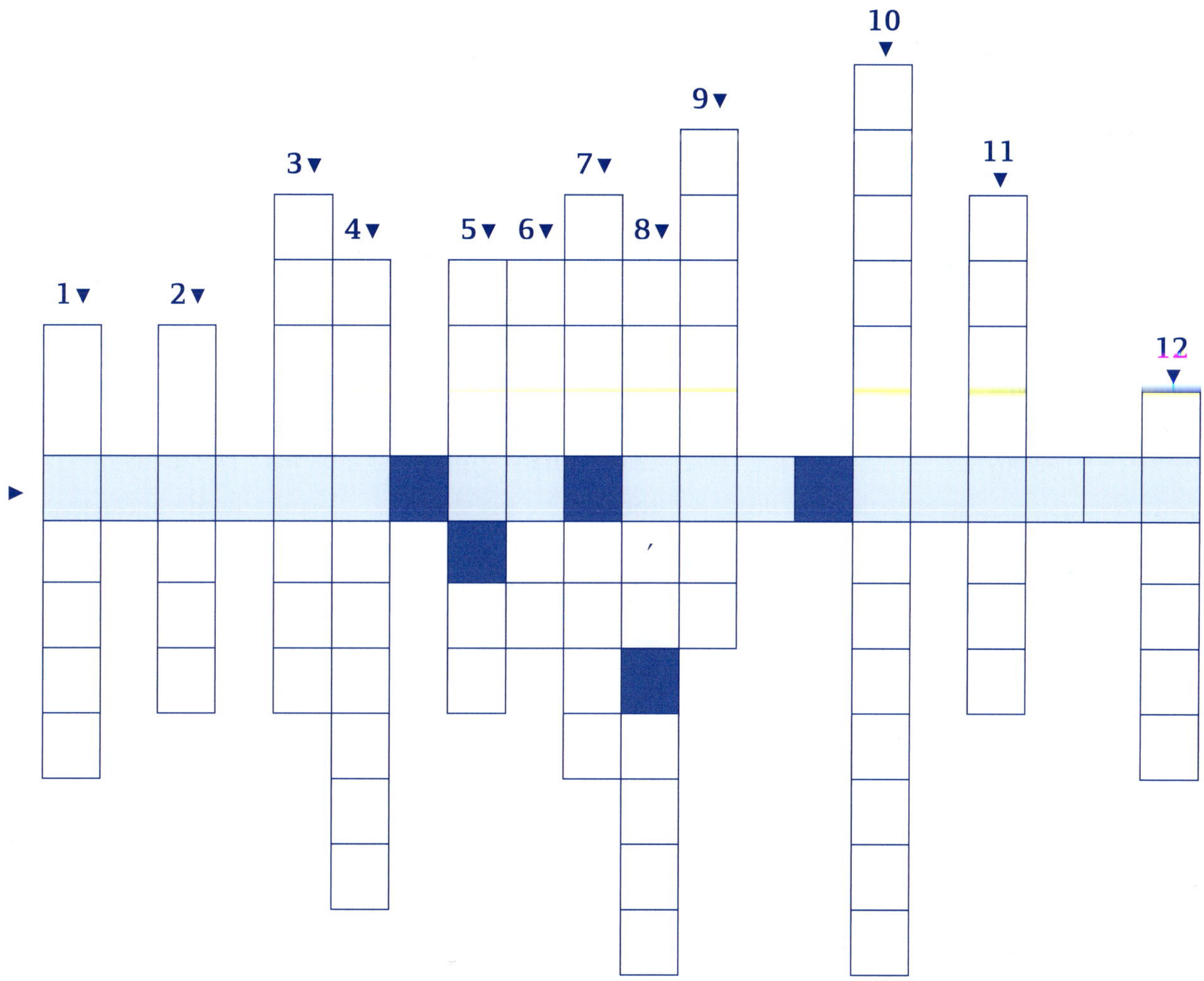

1 It's not easy to ??? the needs of children and the need to earn money.

2 ►► quite

3 proof that something is or isn't true

4 collecting information and putting it together for newspapers or radio or TV reports

5 ►► exactly right

6 Journalists aim to ??? the truth.

7 ►► one more time

8 Fast food can be quite expensive, and ??? ???, it's often not very healthy.

9 When criminals are caught, they are ??? for their crime.

10 sb. who says or does sth. in the name of another person, a company or an organization

11 sb. who has broken the law

12 (to) say that sb. or sth. is very good

11 New words SB p. 66

a) What are the people in the pictures doing? Complete the sentences with the words from the box. Be careful: You have to change the form of the words.

(to) ball • (to) rush • (to) squeeze • (to) stroke • (to) tug • (to) type

1 The boy ______________ ______________ his dog.

2 The woman ______________ the boy by his sleeve.

3 The man ______________ home because it's raining.

4 The woman ______________ a toothpaste tube.

5 The boy ______________ his hand into a fist.

6 The girl ______________ her password into her laptop.

b) Complete the sentences with the words from the box.

anything but • approached • colony • cram • crook • flash freezing • laboratory

1 John often carries his baby in the ______________ of his elbow.

2 ______________ is a process used in the food industry to preserve food.

3 Hong Kong was a British ______________ until 1997.

4 Mara has always been interested in biochemistry and now works in a big ______________.

5 Sara doesn't eat ______________ organically grown fruit and vegetable.

6 "Don't ______________ your clothes into your suitcase, put them in nicely."

7 When Liam ______________ his car, he saw that the front window was broken.

c) What do the following words mean? Match the expressions (A–L) with the corresponding definitions (1–12).

A cryogenic
B cryonics
C grunt
D hiss
E (to) lower
F mortuary
G (to) preserve
H (to) seal sth. (up) with sth.
I speckle
J steam
K tactic
L technician

1 sb. who works with machines or tools
2 ►► (to) let/make sb./sth. go down; (to) reduce
3 (to) keep sth. in a good condition
4 ►► spot (on a differently coloured background)
5 the hot gas that water changes into when it boils
6 involving the use of very low temperatures
7 ►► strategy
8 the sound that a pig makes
9 the technique to freeze a dead body with the hope that it can be brought back to life one day
10 (to) close sth. tightly with sth.
11 the sound that a snake makes
12 a place where dead bodies are kept before they are buried

A	B	C	D	E	F	G	H	I	J	K	L

d) Write the missing words in the crossword.

1 ◄► solid

2 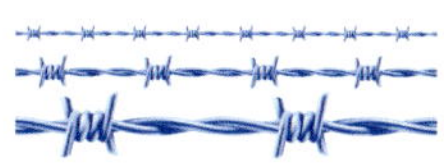

3 a tube in your body that carries blood towards your heart

4 

5 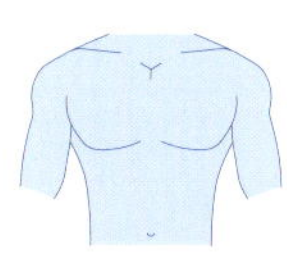

6 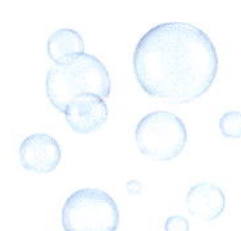

7 

8 

9 

10 

12 New words SB p. 67

a) Look at the illustrations on pp. 60–61 and complete the sentences with the words from the box.

backing down • crops • For Pete's sake! • guilted • insides • intravenous • jerked • needle • point • slammed • stuck • trails

Sue felt she couldn't breathe. So she ran to the window and 1 ________________ it open. It was so hot that her clothes 2 ________________ to her body.

3 " ________________ How can you accept a job in New York? You know that I can't leave London. You could at least have asked me first." – "I'm sorry, Sarah, I see that you have a 4 ________________ there."

"John, you said you'd look after Bobby while we're on holiday, and now you're 5 ________________." – "Well, Mum, you kind of 6 ________________ me into looking after Bobby, but I'm too busy for a dog."

Rain and storm had destroyed all the Miller's 7 ________________. Mrs Miller's 8 ________________ were twisting with fear and 9 ________________ of tears were running down her face.

Tom was so angry with his brother George that he

10 ______________________ the door when he left the room.

Don't worry, Mr Cox. You will hardly feel the

11 ______________________

12 ______________________. I chose a very fine one.

b) What do the following words mean? Match the expressions (A–M) with the corresponding definitions (1–13).

A analyst
B battlefield
C chamber
D command
E genetic
F the military
G mission
H pinky *(AE)*
I puff
J (to) splice
K spine
L (to) undress
M (to) wrap sth. in/with sth.

1 lots of small bones that are connected together and go down the middle of the back
2 ►► order
3 (to) take your clothes off
4 (to) join sth. together, often by twisting the ends together
5 the sound that steam gives off
6 sb. who examines facts or materials in order to give an opinion on them
7 (to) put sth. around sth.
8 a place where two groups of people fight against each other
9 connected with the genes
10 ►► soldiers
11 usually the smallest finger on each hand
12 a place that is almost closed in on all sides
13 an important job that sb. is sent on

A	B	C	D	E	F	G	H	I	J	K	L	M

13 Antonyms

Write the opposites.

1 (to) dress ◄► ______

2 habitable ◄► ______

3 just ◄► ______

4 one-sided ◄► ______

5 open-minded ◄► ______

14 Word families

Use the word given in capitals at the end of each line to form another word of the same word family that fits in the sentence.

1 He ______ his voice as he didn't want to wake the baby.	**LOW**
2 Sue investigates old ______ cases.	**CRIME**
3 The shop sells its goods in ______ containers only.	**REUSE**
4 Our band is looking for a new band ______.	**LEAD**

15 New words SB p. 68

Complete the sentences with the words from the box.

drifts • goes under • solid • splutter • translucent • watery

1 When something is ______, light can get through it, but you can't look through it because it's not really clear.

2 When something is ______, it's hard.

3 When something is ______, it contains a lot of water.

4 When something ______, it could drown.

5 When people or animals ______, they make a series of short noises.

6 When something moves slowly along water, it ______.

16 New words SB p. 69

Write the missing words in the crossword. The clues are on this page and on p. 64.

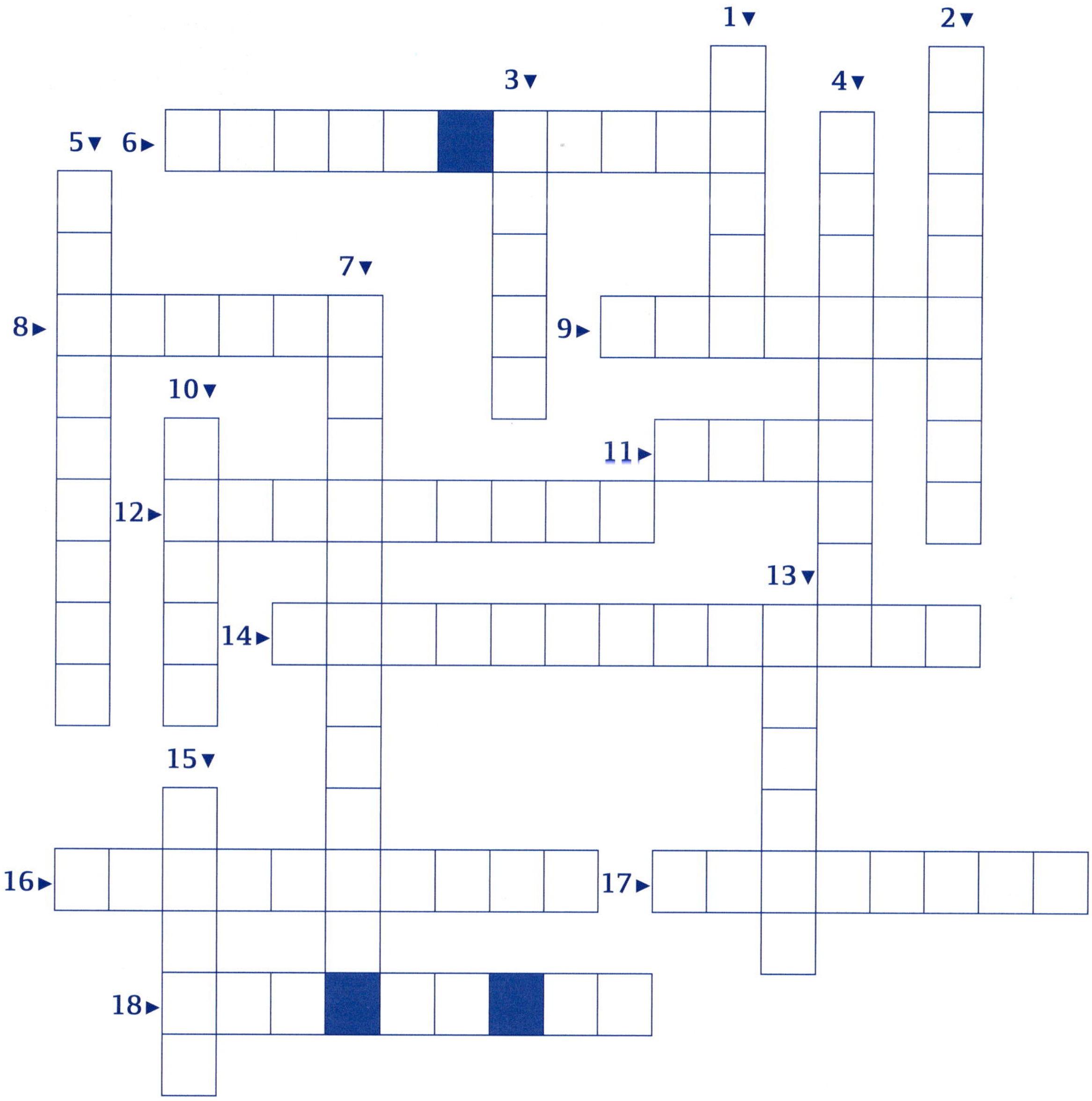

1 the way in which things or people are placed
2 a moving band that is used to transport things from one place to another
3 ►► (to) put (sth. somewhere)
4 a way of doing sth. to achieve a particular purpose
5 (to) move around a certain place
6 energy produced from the sun
7 the study of constructing buildings or machines
8 (to) take away sb./sth. from a particular place
9 ►► *(BE)* rubbish
10 a small piece of sth.
11 part of the sea when it moves
12 wanting to do well or be successful
13 (to) spend money on sth. to make a profit

14 ??? changes have been huge in the last fifty years.
15 a system of different tests
16 ►► %
17 (to) study sth. carefully, often in order to find new facts
18 ►► etc.

17 Synonyms

Choose a word from the box and rewrite each sentence so that it still means the same.

(to) cycle • major • no longer • painful • (to) participate

1 Aisha doesn't work here any more. ______________________

2 Mia doesn't like taking part in discussions. ______________________

3 Sam always rides his bike to work. ______________________

4 Liam's broken leg is causing him lots of pain. ______________________

5 Jake plays an important role in the school play. ______________________

18 Word families: adjectives and nouns

Complete the table with the English and German words.

	adjective	in German	noun	in German
1	extinct			
2		absichtlich, beabsichtigt		
3				Gerechtigkeit

19 New words SB p. 70

Complete the sentences with the words from the box. Be careful: You have to change the form of some of the words.

(to) contribute • (to) expand • (to) group • so far • systematic

Our company **1** ______________ over the last five years and now has over 150 employees. We promise a **2** ______________ approach to building eco-friendly and sustainably. For our new project, all the houses will be **3** ______________ around a small lake. We regularly ask all our employees to **4** ______________ ideas to building sustainable houses that ordinary people can afford. This approach has been very successful **5** ______________.

20 Verbs and prepositions

Complete the sentences with the right preposition.

away • down • for • in • into • on • to • up

1 Whether we can go to the concert will depend ______________ the price of the ticket.

2 Sam felt very sorry ______________ his best friend when he failed the final exam.

3 After her speech lots of students came ______________ to her and congratulated her.

4 He had lied to his parents before, but this time he didn't get ______________ with it.

5 Nora bumped ______________ an old friend of hers when she went into town last week.

6 More and more young people want to get involved ______________ politics.

7 Sue had written a number of emails to Mark, but he never responded ______________ them.

8 We need to cut ______________ on using energy that is not sustainable.

My learner log

Mein Lerntagebuch. Hier notierst du deine Erfahrungen mit dem Wörterlernen.

★ My three favourite words in this unit are:

____

I can …

- express my opinion in different ways in a letter or email. *(Write two examples.)*

____

- group and use words to write about environmental action. *(Write two examples.)*

____

What was difficult in Unit 4:

____

What was easy in Unit 4:

____

What I liked about Unit 4:

____

2 Revision: Units 3 & 4

1 What are they doing?

Write what the people in the pictures are doing.

1 Max *is* ______ his bedroom.

2 The doctor ______ ______ the baby.

3 Some activists ______ ______ a beach.

4 Noel ______ his arms ______ his dad.

5 John ______ his shirt.

6 Lucy ______ her house.

2 Adjectives

Write the seven adjectives next to the correct description or synonym.

ambitious • disadvantaged • essential • frequent • precise • solid • valid

1 exact: ______

2 often: ______

3 hard; not in the form of liquid: ______

4 very important: ______

5 accepted by the system (e.g. a passport): ______

6 wanting to do well or be successful: ______

7 not having things like education, good housing or enough money that help people to succeed in life: ______

3 What are the people saying?

Look at the situation in the pictures and choose a suitable phrase from the box to complete the sentences.

I took it by mistake. • It's not rocket science. • I've got it. • Damn! • There you go! • Yippee!

1 ______________________ I've got the job.

2 Come on, Sam. We can do it. ______________________

3 I passed the driving test! ______________________ I knew you would.

4 I'm sorry. ______________________

5 ______________________ It's easier than I thought.

6 ______________________

4 Word families

Use the word given in capitals at the end of each line to form another word of the same word family that fits in the sentence.

1 Jim suffers from a lack of ______________________.	**CONFIDENT**
2 Give things away if you don't have enough ______________________ space in your house.	**STORE**
3 Children are usually very ______________________.	**ADAPT**
4 A good education is the best ______________________ in your future.	**INVEST**
5 Please turn the ______________________ down to save energy.	**HEAT**

5 Synonyms

a) Draw lines between words or expressions that have a similar meaning.

(to) change sth. completely — (to) produce (goods) — eco-friendly

strategy — (to) tug — rather — meaningful — weird

piece of clothing — environmentally friendly — tactic — quite — (to) pull

(to) manufacture — garment — serious — (to) transform — strange

b) Now use as many of the words as you can to complete the sentences.

1 The way people communicate *has changed completely / transformed* since the invention of the internet.

2 Lots of companies have started to ______________________ things that are sustainable and ______________________.

3 The team has lost all their recent games. Maybe it's time they change their ______________________ ______________________.

4 When Cindy walked into the room, everybody stopped talking. It was ______________________ ______________________ situation.

5 Sam stepped into the road, but someone stopped him by ______________________ him by his arm.

6 Eleanor was looking for a ______________________ job. She found it with an organization that teaches people with disabilities to sew sustainable ______________________.

6 American English – British English

Complete the table.

	AE	BE	German
1			manövrieren, steuern
2		rubbish	
3			im Stadtzentrum Londons

Finale 3

1 A crossword puzzle

Write the missing words in the crossword. Then put the letters in the blue boxes in the right order to form the words for something we need to protect.

1▼ 2▼ 3▶ 4▶ 5▼ 6▼ 7▶ 8▼ 9▶ 10▼ 11▼ 12▶ 13▶ 14▶ 15▶

2

1

3

5

7

8

9

4 any kind of plant that is grown on a farm for food

6 Big building projects are often a threat to the ??? balance of the area.

10 Seals and whales are ??? animals – they live in the sea.

13 ??? areas are areas in the countryside.

14 The natural ??? of the koala is Australia.

11

12

15

Solution: __ __ __   __ __ __ __ __ __

2 The big Go Ahead quiz

Choose the right word or expression in the box, circle the correct letter and follow the arrow (⟶). When you have finished the quiz, read the marked letters from the start to the end.

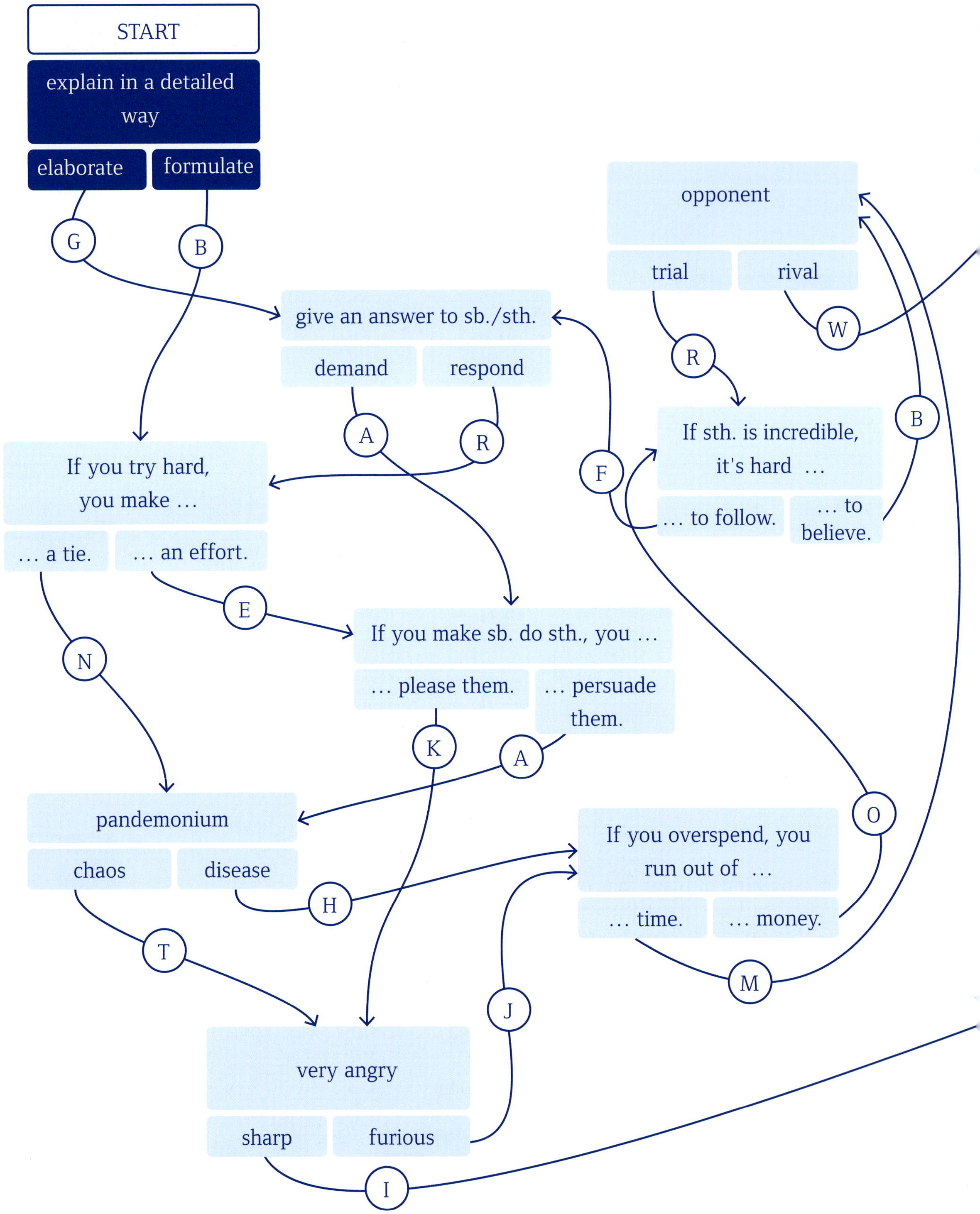

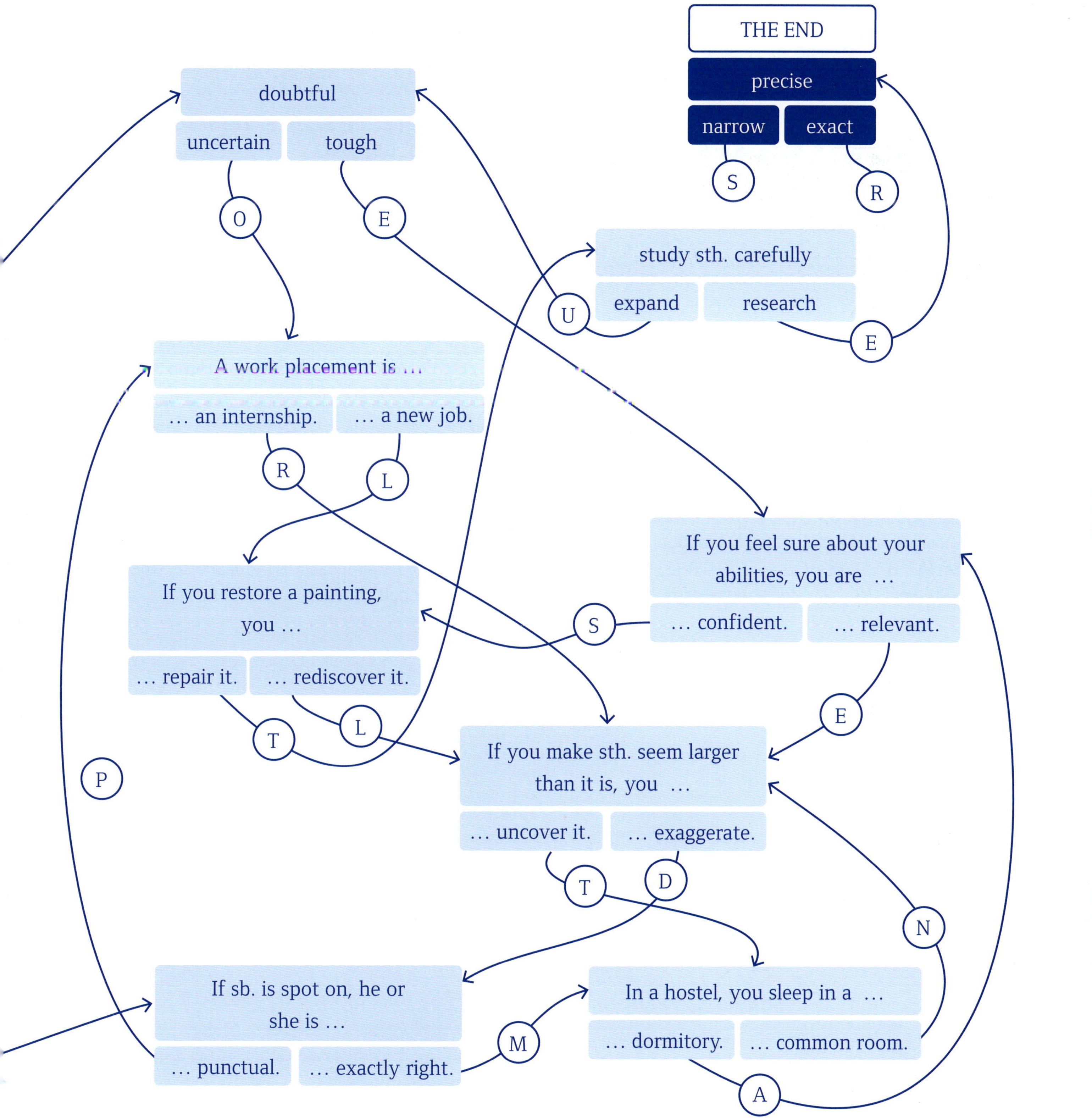
THE END
precise
narrow
exact
S
R
doubtful
uncertain
tough
O
E
study sth. carefully
expand
research
U
E
A work placement is …
… an internship.
… a new job.
R
L
If you feel sure about your abilities, you are …
… confident.
… relevant.
If you restore a painting, you …
… repair it.
… rediscover it.
S
E
T
L
P
If you make sth. seem larger than it is, you …
… uncover it.
… exaggerate.
T
D
N
If sb. is spot on, he or she is …
… punctual.
… exactly right.
M
In a hostel, you sleep in a …
… dormitory.
… common room.
A

_ _ _ _ _ _ _ _ _ _, _ _ _ _ _ _ _ _ _ _ _ _ _ _ _!

Bildquellenverzeichnis

Titelbild: Shutterstock.com/Fabio Principe

Illustrationen
Cornelsen/Karen Donnelly (**S. 8; S. 9** (Nr. 1)**; S. 11; S. 12; S. 16; S. 19; S. 21; S. 23; S. 28; S. 30; S. 33; S. 35; S. 38; S. 47; S. 52; S. 53; S. 55; S. 56; S. 58; S. 60; S. 61; S. 66; S. 67**)

Bildquellen
S. 6: stock.adobe.com/VectorShop; **S. 9** (Nr. 3): stock.adobe.com/slowmotiongli; (Nr. 5): stock.adobe.com/Vaclav Zilvar; (Nr. 12): stock.adobe.com/danmir12; **S. 18:** stock.adobe.com/jodie777; **S. 22** (Nr. 2): stock.adobe.com/Blue Planet Studio; (Nr. 6): Shutterstock.com/Agami Photo Agency; (Nr. 7): Shutterstock.com/Sergey Novikov; **S. 24** (Nr. 1): stock.adobe.com/Ruslan Ivantsov; (Nr. 2): stock.adobe.com/DruZhi Art; (Nr. 3): stock.adobe.com/anatolir; (Nr. 4): Shutterstock.com/Gojindbefs; (Nr. 5): Shutterstock.com/Jemastock; (Nr. 6): Shutterstock.com/SaveJungle; **S. 40** (links): stock.adobe.com/radiokafka; (Mitte): stock.adobe.com/Tony Ruji; (rechts): stock.adobe.com/robynmac; **S. 41** (oben): stock.adobe.com/soft_light; (unten): stock.adobe.com/Berni; **S. 43:** stock.adobe.com/Sashkin; **S. 45:** stock.adobe.com/indigolotos; **S. 51:** stock.adobe.com/puckillustrations; **S. 59** (Nr. 2): Shutterstock.com/Natykach Nataliia; (Nr. 4): Shutterstock.com/Olga Popova; (Nr. 5): Shutterstock.com/Ed123; (Nr. 6): Shutterstock.com/ILYA AKINSHIN; (Nr. 7): Shutterstock.com/smartman; (Nr. 8): Shutterstock.com/Anton Starikov; (Nr. 9): Shutterstock.com/nikiteev_konstantin; (Nr. 10): stock.adobe.com/eurobanks; **S. 62:** stock.adobe.com/tobago77; **S. 69** (Nr. 1): stock.adobe.com/ricardoreitmeyer; (Nr. 2): stock.adobe.com/Michael Robbins; (Nr. 3): stock.adobe.com/JohanSwanepoel; (Nr. 5): stock.adobe.com/elenavolf; (Nr. 7): stock.adobe.com/Eric Isselée; (Nr. 8): Shutterstock.com/JT888; (Nr. 9): Shutterstock.com/Edy Pamungkas; (Nr. 11): Shutterstock.com/Olga Altunina; (Nr. 12): stock.adobe.com/Joseph; (Nr. 15): Shutterstock.com/Andrei F